RICHARD SOPRIS IN EARLY DENVER

RICHARD SOPRIS IN EARLY DENVER

Captain, Mayor & Colorado Fifty-Niner

Linda Bjorklund

Foreword by Dr. Thomas Noel

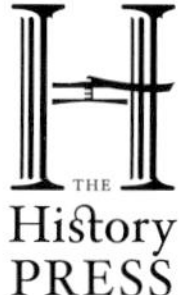

Published by The History Press
Charleston, SC
www.historypress.net

First published 2016

Manufactured in the United States

ISBN 978.1.46713.593.1

Library of Congress Control Number: 2016931934

Contents

Foreword, by Dr. Thomas Noel 7
Preface 9

1. From Yardley to Michigan City 11
2. Hunt for Gold 16
3. Kansas Legislature and Provisional Territorial Government 27
4. Mount Sopris 33
5. Bummers 40
6. Glorieta Pass 48
7. Agriculture, Floods and Locusts 55
8. Sheriff Sopris 62
9. Railroad Contractor 68
10. Warden Sopris; Colorado Is a State 75
11. Mayor Sopris 80
12. Denver's City Park 87
13. The Rest of the Family 92
14. Sopris the Town 107
15. State Historical Society 111
16. And the Family Tree Grows 115

Bibliography 123
Index 135
About the Author 139

Foreword

In May 2011, CU-Denver History Professor Tom Noel—known locally as Dr. Colorado for his research, teaching, tours and writings about the history of the Highest State—submitted to the *Denver Post* a column with the title "Denver's next mayor has big shoes to fill." In the article, Dr. Noel listed five former Denver mayors he reckoned to be the city's top mayors throughout its history. The first one listed was Richard Sopris, mayor from 1878 to 1881.

> *Sopris first championed Denver's now superb park system and is commemorated by Sopris Gate at City Park. A Pennsylvania farm boy who became a Mississippi riverboat pilot and also built submarines, Sopris joined the 1859 gold rush to Colorado. He helped establish Glenwood Springs and is honored by nearby Mount Sopris. Captain Sopris also helped found the Society of Colorado Pioneers, an ancestor of today's History Colorado.*

Asked to comment on *Richard Sopris in Early Denver: Captain, Mayor & Colorado Fifty-Niner*, Dr. Noel responded:

> *Richard Sopris was a part of the history of the State of Colorado and the City of Denver, usually in the thick of things or at least on the edge of things as one of the first gold miners and explorers, then as Mayor of Denver from 1878–1881 and then as Denver's pioneer*

park commissioner. Linda Bjorklund's book delves into the details of this fascinating and ubiquitous, but underappreciated pioneer crucial to Colorado and its capital city.

Preface

This book is so much more than the history of one man, Captain Richard Sopris. Ms. Bjorklund researched, gathered and discovered so many facets and stories of early Denver, Colorado, and national events of the times about which she wrote that she managed to weave a wonderful historical story of the life and times of Captain Sopris. Our family shall ever be grateful to Linda for putting our ancestor's life into words for us all to relish.

Margaret (Peg) Farrington Hulsey
Great-great-great-granddaughter of Richard Sopris

I

From Yardley to Michigan City

Richard Sopris was born in Yardley, Bucks County, Pennsylvania, on July 26, 1813, son of James and Mary Sopris. William Penn, founder of the state of Pennsylvania, named the county after Buckinghamshire, his home county in England. Bucks County was one of the three original counties in the American colony.

The town of Yardley is situated a few miles from the Delaware River and not too far from Philadelphia. This is where George Washington crossed the Delaware on Christmas Day 1776. Washington's troops had been defeated by the British at several locations, and morale was at a low ebb. Thomas Payne was prompted to write, "These are the times that try men's souls." Washington had taken his men to the Pennsylvania side of the Delaware River to regroup in an area near the town of Yardley. The Hessians, Germans hired by the British,

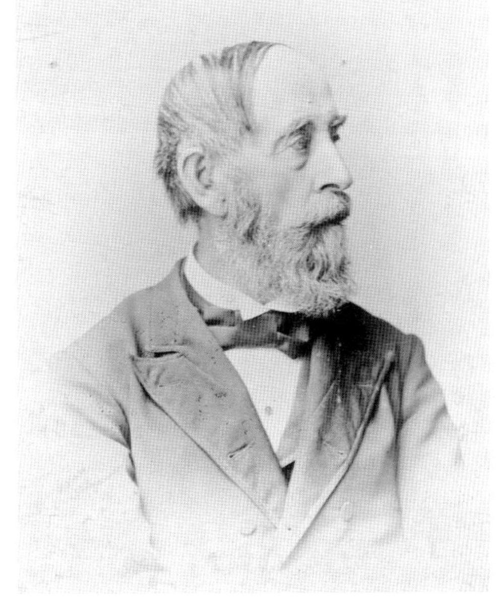

Richard Sopris. *Courtesy of the Farrington family.*

were camped in Trenton, New Jersey, on the opposite shore of the Delaware and had been celebrating their military victories, as well as Christmas Day festivities. Washington loaded a number of freight hauling–type boats with his troops, and during the frigid night, they quietly made their way across the river. The plan was to disembark on the New Jersey side of the river and flank the Hessians from both the north and south of their camp to overcome them, which the Americans successfully accomplished. The victory provided a well-needed boost to the morale of the patriot soldiers.

Richard Sopris grew up here and worked on his father's farm until he was sixteen years old. He then began to learn the trade of house carpenter. He met Elizabeth Allen, a descendant of the patriot Ethan Allen, in Trenton and married her on June 5, 1836. The couple moved to Brookville, Indiana, where Sopris became a contractor on the Whitewater Canal.

Canal building has been going on since humans decided they needed to travel and found floating on a waterway much easier than walking or urging a horse along a rough path. Earliest canals were depicted on clay tablets, showing short waterways connecting to the Euphrates River in ancient Mesopotamia.

In the United States, having won the Revolutionary War, citizens began to look inward for ways to connect with one another. Numerous waterways prompted notables like George Washington to organize the building of canals to encourage commerce in the young nation. The success of early canal building led to a major undertaking across the state of New York.

Pioneers had moved westward and settled along the banks of the Great Lakes. They were able to establish a lucrative trade with Canadians but were prohibited from dealing with their own countrymen on the East Coast because of the difficult path across the Appalachian Mountains. Those coming into New York Harbor found the going easy up the Hudson River until they reached Albany. What forward-looking enthusiasts envisioned was a waterway system that connected Albany with Buffalo, located on the banks of Lake Erie.

It took nearly nearly nine years of construction to complete the canal, but in 1825, when it was ready to be used, New York Governor DeWitt Clinton boarded a vessel named the *Seneca Chief* in Buffalo. The vessel made its way to New York City carrying a cask of Lake Erie water, which the governor poured into New York Harbor. This was the momentous opening of the Erie Canal.

Success of the Erie Canal prompted state governments in Ohio and Pennsylvania to build their own canal systems. The Ohio River flows out of Pennsylvania westward, forming the southern boundaries of the

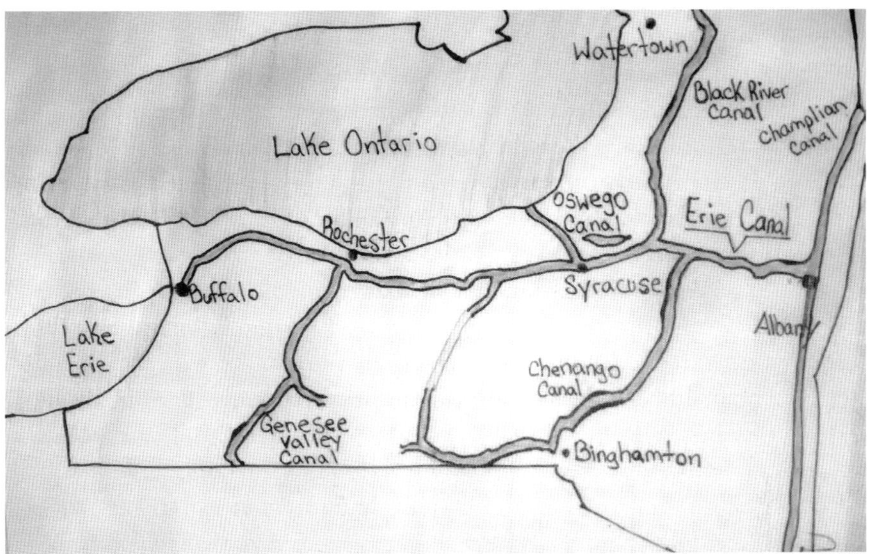

Erie Canal. *Drawing by Angie Hopkins.*

states of Ohio and Indiana and the southeastern boundary of Illinois. The Ohio River meets and flows into the Missouri River at the southern tip of central Illinois.

The State of Indiana was eager to share in the wealth created by the canal systems. Its neighboring State of Ohio had built two major canal systems, the Ohio-Erie and the Miami-Erie. The Ohio-Erie connected Lake Erie at Cleveland with the Ohio River at Portsmouth. The Miami-Erie connected Lake Erie at Toledo to the Ohio River at Cincinnati. Engineers in the state of Indiana proposed two canal systems. The Wabash and Erie Canal was to connect with the Miami-Erie in Ohio and follow the Wabash River westward across the state of Indiana, veering southward as it flowed into the Ohio River. The Whitewater Canal was to extend southward from Hagerstown in eastern Indiana along the Whitewater River, through Brookville, flowing into the Ohio River at Lawrenceburg.

The Indiana State Legislature passed the Mammoth Internal Improvement Act in 1836, and construction on both projects began. Unfortunately, progress was diminished when a nationwide economic downturn in 1837 severely crippled the availability of funds. The state finished the Wabash and Erie Canal in 1843 but was forced to turn the canal system over to its creditors. The Whitewater Canal system was turned over to a private company in 1842 and was finally finished in 1847.

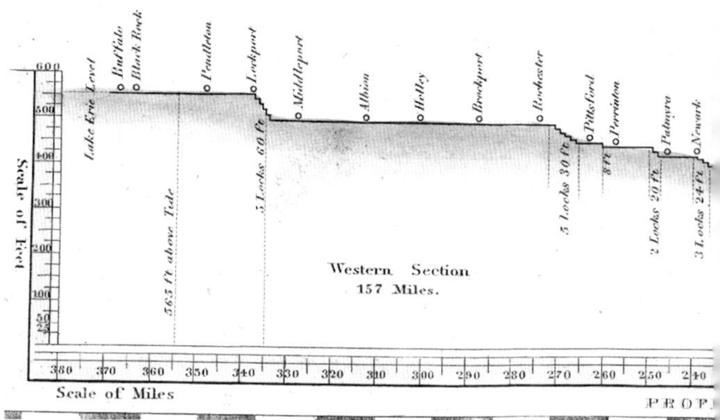

Right: An 1832 Erie Canal map. *PD-US.*

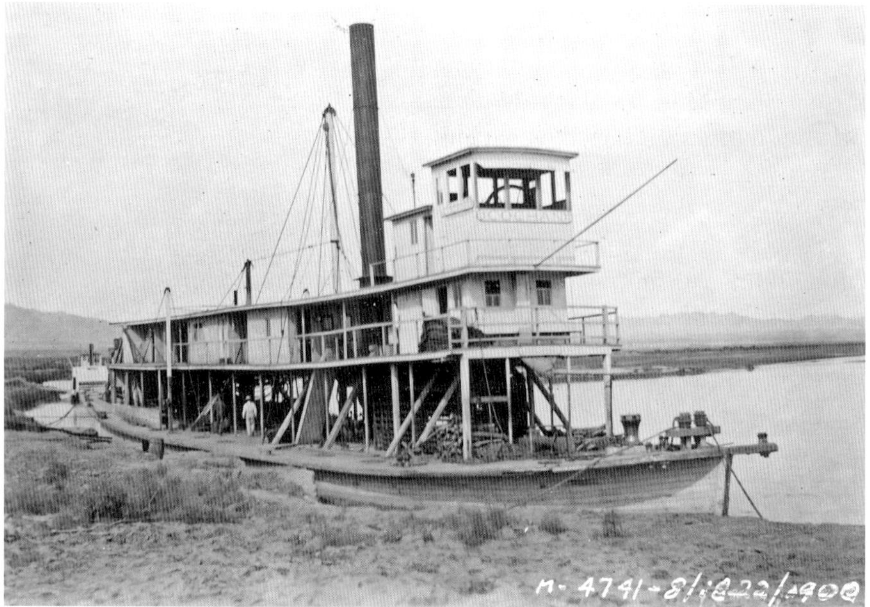

Below: A view showing the steamboat *Cochan* on the Colorado River near Yuma, Arizona. This picture was taken in 1900 by L.C. Easton. *Courtesy of the U.S. National Archives and Records Administration.*

Richard Sopris was a contractor during the construction phase of the Whitewater Canal. As they were completed, the canal systems began to be used, and Sopris became captain of an Ohio River steamer in 1840. His boat was called the *Indiana*. His steamboat route followed the river systems from Cincinnati to New Orleans.

Steamboats revolutionized river travel in the late 1700s and early 1800s. Powered by steam, the riverboats could travel at the astonishing speed of five miles per hour. But the dangers of steamboat travel began to overtake the advantages. If not carefully maintained, a boiler could build up

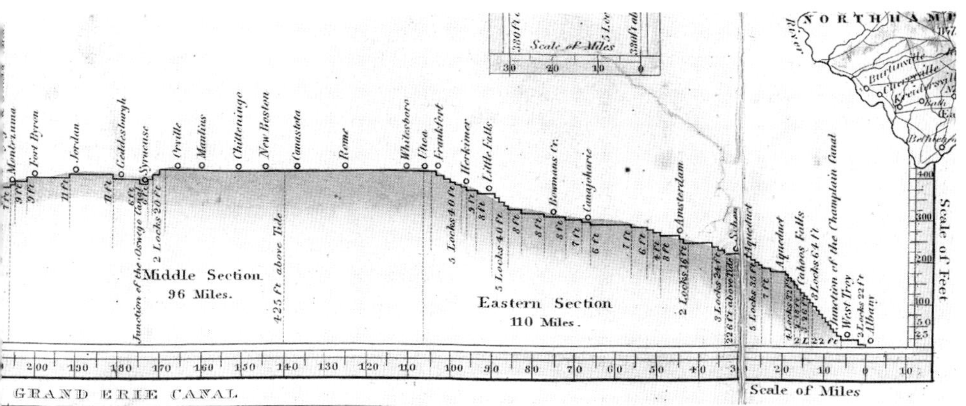

pressure that resulted in a destructive explosion. If the steamboat became incapacitated, Indians along the river banks could easily attack the boat and its passengers. But one of the worst dangers was the tendency of the captains to challenge one another to races. While exciting to watch, these activities put the passengers and crews in serious danger.

The era of the steamboat began to wane when railroads emerged as a viable travel option. After serving a five-year stint as a riverboat captain, Sopris took up railroad contracting and building. He became interested in opening an iron foundry in Michigan City, Indiana, and moved the family there. While working the foundry, he spent time submarine diving along the shores of Lake Michigan.

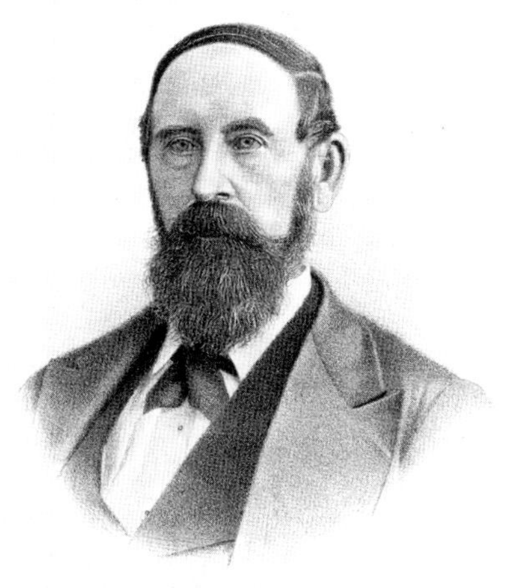

Richard Sopris. *Courtesy of the Farrington family.*

During the time Richard and his wife, Elizabeth, lived in Indiana, eight children were born to them: Allen B. was born in 1837; Indiana was born in 1839; Irene was born in 1841; Elbridge B. was born in 1843; Simpson T. was born in 1845; Henry C. was born in 1847; Levi S. was born in 1850; and George L. was born in 1853.

The foundry business was only moderately successful, and eight children needed to be fed, clothed and educated. In 1859, Sopris heard about gold discoveries in the Pikes Peak region of Colorado.

2

Hunt for Gold

William Greeneberry Russell grew up in Georgia, the son of a gold miner who was active in the 1828 Georgia gold rush. In 1845, William married a woman who was part Cherokee Indian. When news of the 1849 California gold rush became known, he and his two brothers, Joseph and Levi, went west along with a band of Cherokees. On their way, they traveled through the Rocky Mountains in what would later be Colorado and tried their luck prospecting in a few mountain streams. They found a bit of color but continued to California to the gold fields that were by now well known.

Moderately successful, the brothers and their band of Cherokees returned home to Georgia. Then they heard the rumors of the Pikes Peak gold discovery. And they remembered the trace of gold they had found. The Russell brothers again headed west and were joined by a band of Cherokees, as well as some Kansans. Their party numbered over a hundred. They reached Cherry Creek and followed it north to its confluence with the South Platte River, where they set up camp. The date was June 24, 1858.

The Russell party searched up and down the South Platte looking for signs of a bonanza of gold. They followed several of the creeks that originated in the mountains and emptied into the South Platte. Then they found a gold deposit on Little Dry Creek that yielded enough to prompt them to stay and continue with placer mining.

While William and Joseph were canvassing the mountain streams for gold, their brother Levi, who was a physician, stayed at the campsite that they had established between Cherry Creek and the South Platte River.

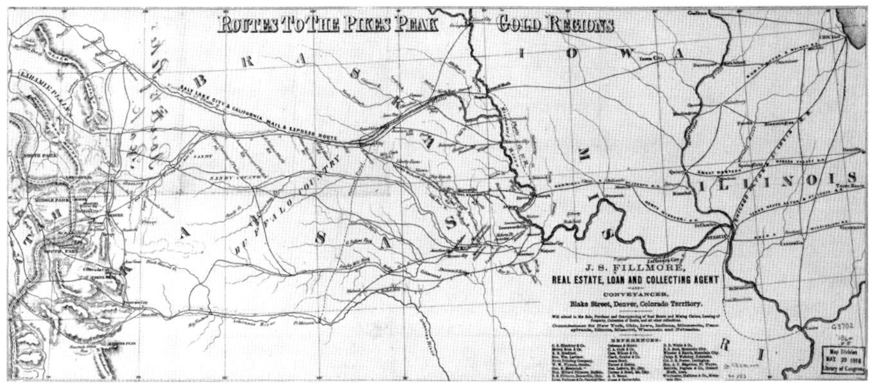

A map of the routes to the Pikes Peak gold fields, circa 1861. It was commissioned by J.S. Fillmore, a land speculator and merchant. *Courtesy of the Library of Congress Maps Division.*

The campsite became a townsite when several other men got involved and decided to establish the Auraria Town Company. A committee was appointed to draft a constitution and bylaws. Anyone who built a house at least sixteen by sixteen feet was eligible to be a stockholder in the company. The constitution was approved on November 1, 1858, and shortly thereafter William McFadding was elected president and Dr. Levi Russell secretary of the organization.

The land involved was described as "a tract having Cherry Creek for the Easterly line and the South Platte for the northerly line and extending west and south sufficiently to include not less than six hundred and forty acres." William McGaw (Mcgaa) and John S. Smith were given the exclusive right to maintain a ferry landing on the river within the boundaries of the townsite. The name "Auraria" was suggested by Dr. Russell after his hometown in Georgia, where there were also gold diggings.

Meanwhile, on the east side of Cherry Creek, across from the Auraria settlement, a group of men that had come from Lawrence, Kansas, staked out a mile-square tract of land in the vicinity of where 14th Street and Blake Street are now. They voted on a constitution for the St. Charles Town Association and elected officers. In October 1858, the men in the group thought they had better get the townsite approved by the legislature of the Kansas Territory to make everything legal. They headed east, but a few days out they decided that someone should stay back and protect their claim, so Charles Nichols turned around and went back to the site. He attempted to begin construction of a cabin by laying out four logs, which was the normal way to establish a claim.

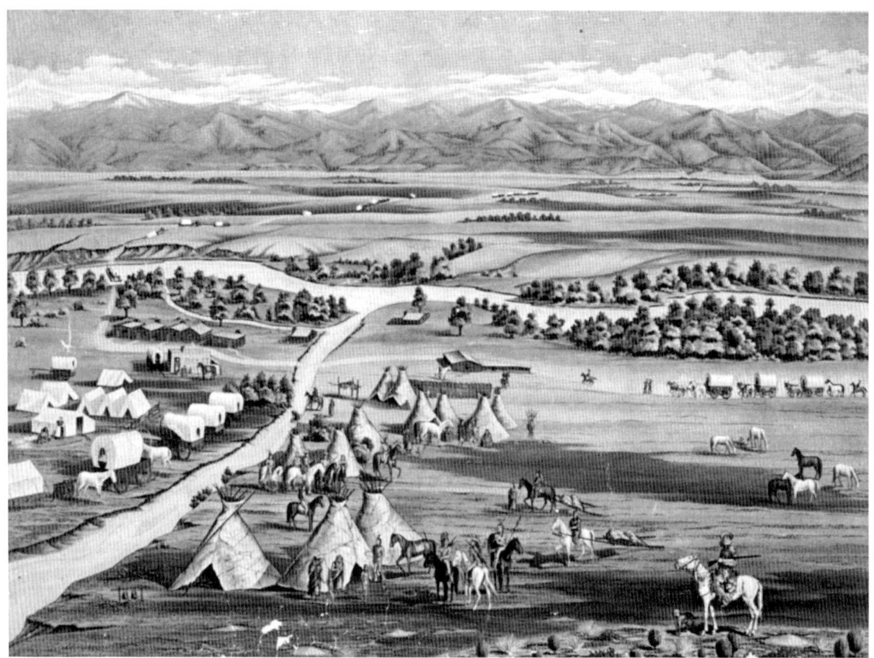

Denver in 1859. Made by Collier & Cleveland Litho Co., circa April 21, 1891. *Courtesy of the Library of Congress Prints and Photographs Division, Washington, D.C.*

In mid-November, another group of men, this time from Leavenworth, Kansas, arrived at the Cherry Creek site. They had the foresight to bring with them authorization from the legislature of the Kansas Territory, appointing officers of the town from among their members. They quickly discovered the attempt of Nichols to claim the property and overwhelmed him, effectively jumping the claim of the Lawrence group.

The Denver City Town Company passed its own constitution on November 22, 1858, and began to build homes and businesses on the site. Members of the St. Charles Town Association were given shares in the new town, which was named after the governor of Kansas Territory, James W. Denver.

Back in Indiana, Captain Sopris became intrigued by the news of the gold findings in the Pikes Peak area. He left his wife, Elizabeth, and their eight children in Indiana while he traveled west to see if there was a future in the gold fields for them. He arrived in the Cherry Creek area in March 1859. By that time, there were about a hundred houses and a number of businesses between the towns of Auraria and Denver. In April, Sopris headed up into the mountains to try his luck at finding gold. He followed the South Platte

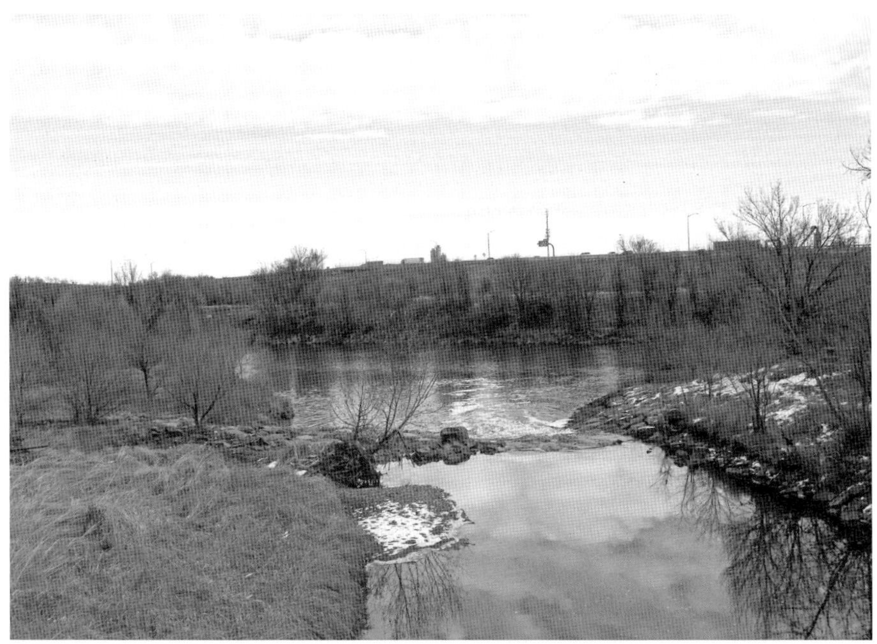

Clear Creek where it empties into the South Platte River. *Photo by author.*

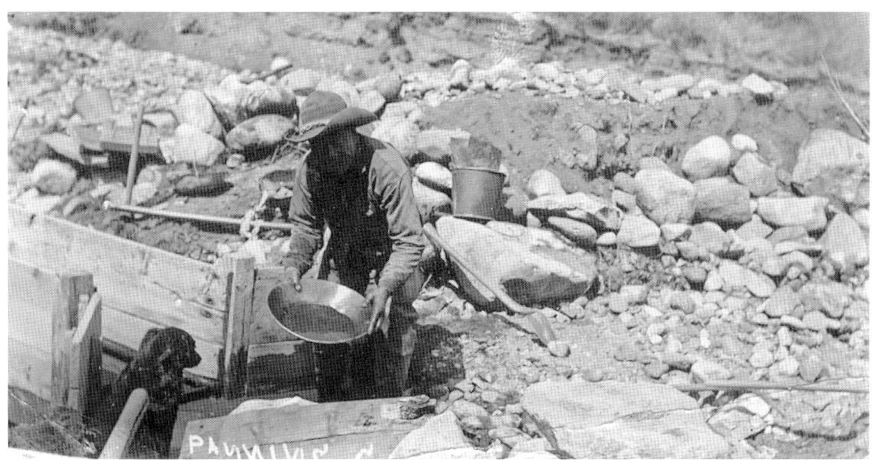

Gold panning. *Courtesy the of Park County Local History Archives.*

River, then Clear Creek where the two merge, and set up camp near the area that later became Central City.

Sopris began to try some placer mining in the area, looking for gold near a source of water. That same month, a visitor came to his camp.

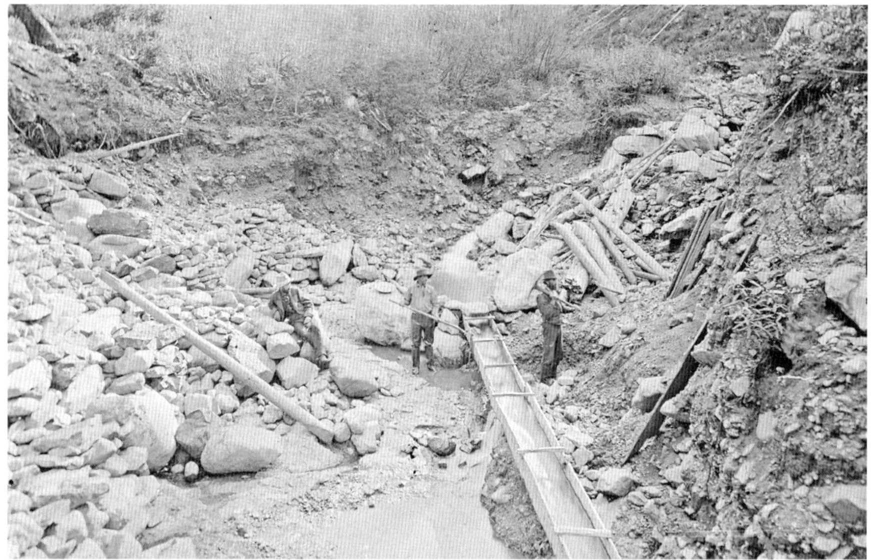

Sluicing for gold in Boren's Gulch. *Photo by the U.S. Geological and Geographic Survey of the Territories. Courtesy of the U.S. National Archives and Records Administration.*

The visitor was John H. Gregory, an experienced miner from Georgia. Sopris had been looking for gold in the creek but had not found it in paying quantities.

Gregory explained that the gold in the streams was only a small portion of the gold hidden in mountain crevices. Sopris was fascinated to find out that the source of the gold that made its way to the mountain streams was actually deep in the mountains. Gregory looked for likely rock formations containing "rotting" quartz that would indicate a seam of gold. He patiently explained to Sopris the concept of lode mining. Instead of panning for gold nuggets in streams of water—the procedure for placer mining—the prospector would use a pick and shovel to dig up the earth, carry it to a sluice or receptacle with slats built into it and pour water over it. The water would flow down the sluice, carrying the lighter materials with it, leaving the heavier gold behind the slats to be picked out and taken elsewhere for further refinement.

Gregory had located a ridge in the area that he thought was likely to contain a gold lode. He convinced Sopris and a number of other miners to work the lode, which came to be known as Gregory's Diggings. This lode eventually would yield millions of dollars of gold.

Not far away, another prospector, George A. Jackson, struck out on his own up Clear Creek and discovered a similar outcropping of gold near a hot

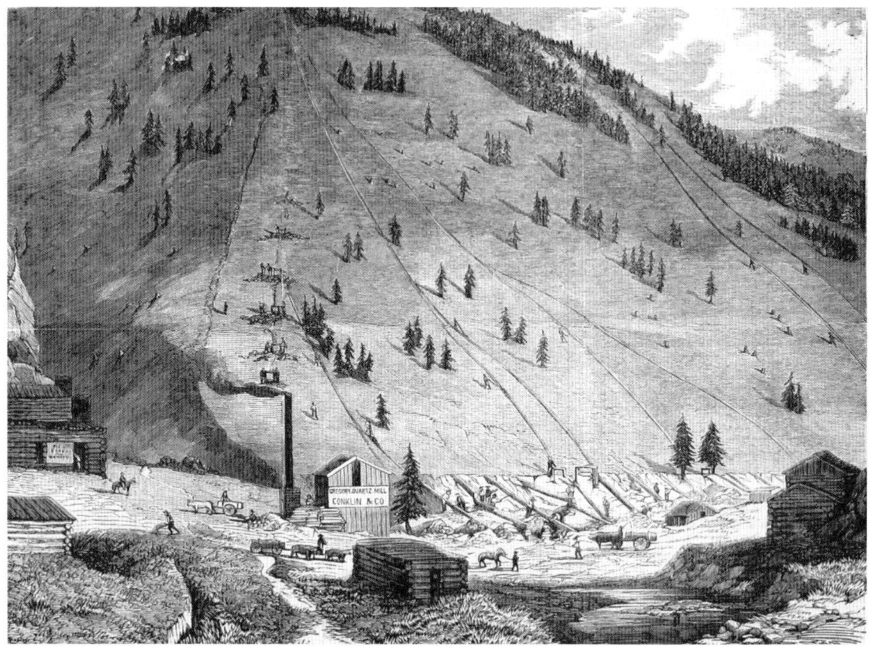

"Sketch of Gregory's Quartz Mill, Pikes Peak, Made on the Spot by Col. D.H. Huyett, Expressly for *Frank Leslie's Illustrated Newspaper*." *From* Frank Leslie's Illustrated Newspaper, *December 15, 1860.*

mineral springs. A town was later established in this area that we now know as Idaho Springs.

Captain Sopris became acquainted with Green Russell in May 1859. The two of them went with two other prospectors southeast from Gregory's Diggings until Russell found a ravine coming out of the mountains and said there would be good diggings there. They promptly named it Russells Gulch, and his prediction later turned out to be true. Sopris described Russell as a large man, about six feet tall, who wore his beard very long. Russell would plait the beard and stick it inside his shirt to keep it out of the way. Sopris further described him as a very quiet man with not much education, but a practical miner.

But Sopris and other miners continued to work at Gregory's Diggings. In May, they began to build cabins to live in and called their town Mountain City. Mining camps filled the area near Clear Creek up and down the steep mountainside called Gregory Gulch. At the bottom of the gulch, a town developed with mills and refineries. It was called Black Hawk. Farther up the gulch, the town of Mountain City was laid out, about halfway between

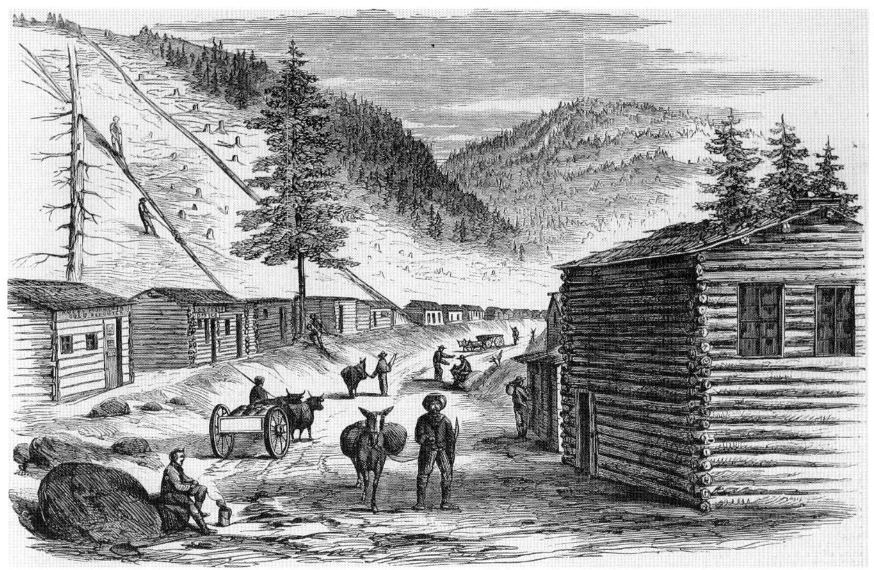

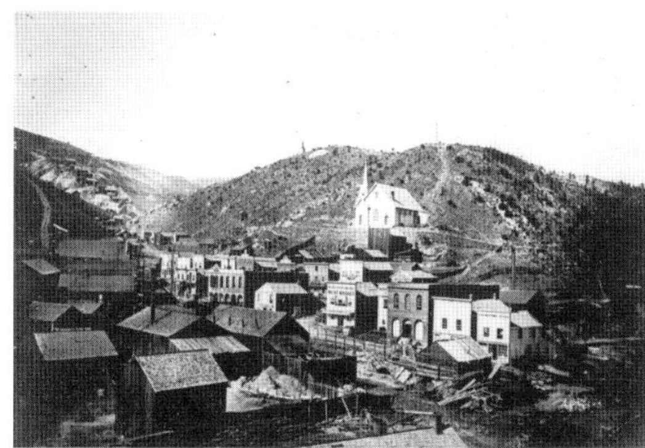

Above: "Street in Gregory Gilch, Pikes Peak—From Sketch Made on The Spot, Expressly for *Frank Leslie's Illustrated Newspaper*, by Col. D.H. Huyett." *From* Frank Leslie's Illustrated Newspaper, *December 15, 1860.*

Left: Black Hawk Company, 1864. *George D. Wakely, PD-US.*

Black Hawk and the town of Central City. In addition to the log cabins, tents and brush shacks, a commercial area boasted a tent hotel and a log theater. A Masonic Hall and two newspapers took up residence there. A church began to hold services in June. And of course, a mountain saloon dispensed liquor of dubious quality from unwashed tin cups.

From a diary written by Joseph Persons Jr., one of the inhabitants was identified:

> *Sunday, June 19, 1859*
> *There is preaching every Sabbath at Mountain City. It is a very peaceable place for so many men. There is in the mountains now about seven thousand*

men and one woman. Her name is Charley. She dresses in black pants, hickory shirt, vest and moccasins. Her pants project well behind. Her vest does not want any batting either.

The woman described in Persons' diary was a unique character referred to as "Mountain Charley." One version of her background is that she came from Iowa, where she was known as Charlotte. She had married a fellow who was not only a professional gambler but did not regard fidelity as one of his attributes. When he took off for the Colorado gold fields with another woman, Charlotte followed them to Mountain City and "exacted her revenge." She then left the Mountain City community and later enlisted with an Iowa regiment during the Civil War disguised as a man. She managed to penetrate Confederate lines as a spy under the guise of a male orderly. After the war ended, Charlotte resumed a more normal life and settled down to raise a family far from Mountain City.

Another version of Mountain Charley's identity is that her name was actually Elsa Jane Forest, and she was prospecting at Gregory's Diggings but also looking for the man who had killed her husband on a Mississippi riverboat. Horace Greeley met her while he was at Mountain City and noticed that her voice was too feminine to be a man's. Greeley observed her "smoking, drinking, swearing, and taking equal parts in the amusements of a crowd of loafers." Another acquaintance said that she was "always armed with a revolver or two in her belt and a long sheath-knife in her boot-leg." Not finding the man she was looking for, Elsa left. She apparently ran into him five years later, at which time they exchanged gunfire.

The town of Mountain City eventually was absorbed by Central City. There is now a historical marker to show the location of the Gregory Diggings site.

Richard Sopris filed a claim with a partner on the Bates lode. Sopris, Henderson & Company ran a sluice six days a week using four men: one to dig, one to carry and two to wash. One report recorded the production at $607 for a week's work.

Sopris recalled first meeting William Byers in a tent at Mountain City. Born in Ohio in 1831, Byers spent his youth learning to farm. To pursue a better education, he attended an academy in Ohio, where he trained in the art of land surveying. After years of following that profession in Washington, Oregon and California, he took the route back across the Isthmus of Panama (before the canal) and ended up in Omaha, Nebraska. He attempted to resume his trade as surveyor and real estate agent until he was

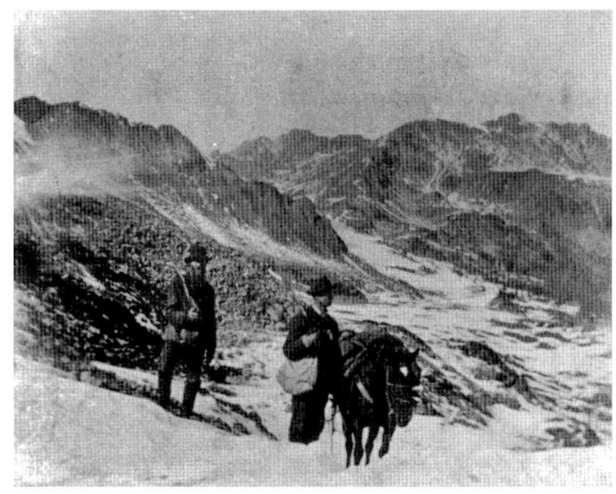

Prospectors in what was then the Pikes Peak region of western Kansas Territory (modern Colorado), circa 1858. *PD-US.*

temporarily incapacitated in a street brawl. He began to write about his experiences in traveling and in the gold fields. He compiled his writings with other newspaper accounts of happenings in the gold fields and published the manuscript as a guidebook. Its success convinced Byers that he should start up a newspaper in the Pikes Peak region.

Byers partnered with an Omaha editor and a skilled printer, and they named the *Rocky Mountain News* before they even left Nebraska. They loaded up the printing press and paper into a wagon and headed west. They reached Denver and looked over a few lots that were offered them for the newspaper office. Byers opted, however, to locate in a rickety building across Cherry Creek in the town of Auraria. He hurriedly published his first edition after the press was hauled up the stairs and a tent erected over it to divert rain from a leaking roof. The first *Rocky Mountain News* hit the streets on April 23, 1859.

Byers could sense where the mining news would be and headed to the site of Gregory's Diggings, where the most recent gold find was reported. He was joined by other notable newspaper editors of the time, among them Horace Greeley of the *New York Tribune.*

Greeley had boarded the Leavenworth and Pikes Peak Express Company stagecoach at Manhattan, Kansas. The fledgling stagecoach line had begun service a few months prior and took seven days to travel the 687 miles to Denver. Along the way, the stagecoach suffered a mishap that left Greeley injured. The stagecoach was pulled by four mules that were surprised by the sudden appearance of three Indians just as the coach was descending an abrupt hill. The mules stampeded and the coach overturned, leaving the occupants underneath a pile of the remains. Greeley's wounds were treated by a woman at the next station, but he continued to limp for a good year afterward.

The stagecoach arrived in Denver on June 6, 1859. Undaunted by his injuries, Greeley stayed in Denver long enough to give a speech to

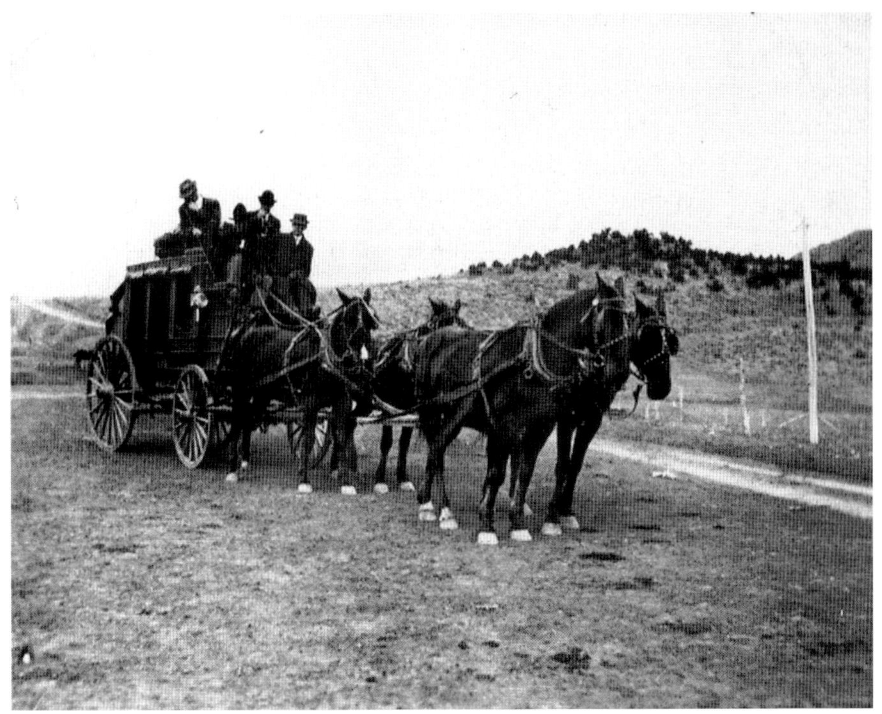

A stagecoach. *Courtesy of the Park County Local History Archives.*

the drinking patrons at the Denver House Hotel. A devout believer in temperance, he loudly proclaimed the evils of drinking and gambling and castigated the resident ladies of the night. His speech was greeted with cheers and applause and the stamping of feet, immediately after which the local patrons resumed their previous activities.

On June 8, Greeley and other newsmen set out to visit Gregory's Diggings so they could report on the gold findings. They rode in wagons as far as the foothills, then mounted mules for the rest of the journey. As they crossed Clear Creek, running unusually high for the season, Greeley's mule began floundering as he tried to swim. The others soon rescued the beleaguered newsman, and they arrived at Mountain City safely.

Greeley again gave his anti-drinking, anti-gambling speech at the log hotel in Mountain City. Meanwhile, the miners, eager to impress newspaper readers back east, had used a dry hole to "salt" with shotgun blasts full of gold dust. This was a tactic used by many a miner who was tired of digging and wanted to sell his claim. In his report, Greeley dutifully reported the gold finds but cited the difficulty and expense of mining, the scarcity of water and the hard winters that preclude successful efforts at bringing out gold. But in spite of the negatives, his readers were encouraged with the advice, "Go West, Young Man!"

3

Kansas Legislature and Provisional Territorial Government

Richard Sopris continued to work at the Gregory Diggings. Recognizing the need for a water source, he helped organize a ditch company to divert water for their use. The Missouri City Ditch was eleven miles long and brought water to the area. Miners began to use newfangled devices to help free the gold from other materials. An arrastra was used to crush the ore by means of heavy rocks dragged over the ore by burros or mules. Water was needed to wash the unwanted material away, leaving the gold. Another device called a "woodpecker mill" was an iron-shod wooden trip hammer. The mill was powered by a flow of water that carried the materials into a wooden, iron-lined trough. The heavier gold was caught and separated while the lighter-weight materials were washed down the trough. Stamp mills were built to crush the ore so gold could more easily be separated. Again, water was needed to power the mills and wash the lighter-weight materials away.

June 1859 was extremely dry, and the accumulation of woodland debris was as inflammable as tinder. It was reported that a destructive fire had been raging amongst the pines for the previous week. On the fifteenth of the month, a miner found bodies of three men, a pony and a dog that had succumbed to the fire. Captain Sopris was one of a dozen men called upon to investigate the tragic deaths. The bodies were so badly burned that there was no way to identify them. The few possessions found near them indicated that they were miners, and the articles were gathered to be held in Mountain City just in case someone might be able to recognize the victims by their belongings.

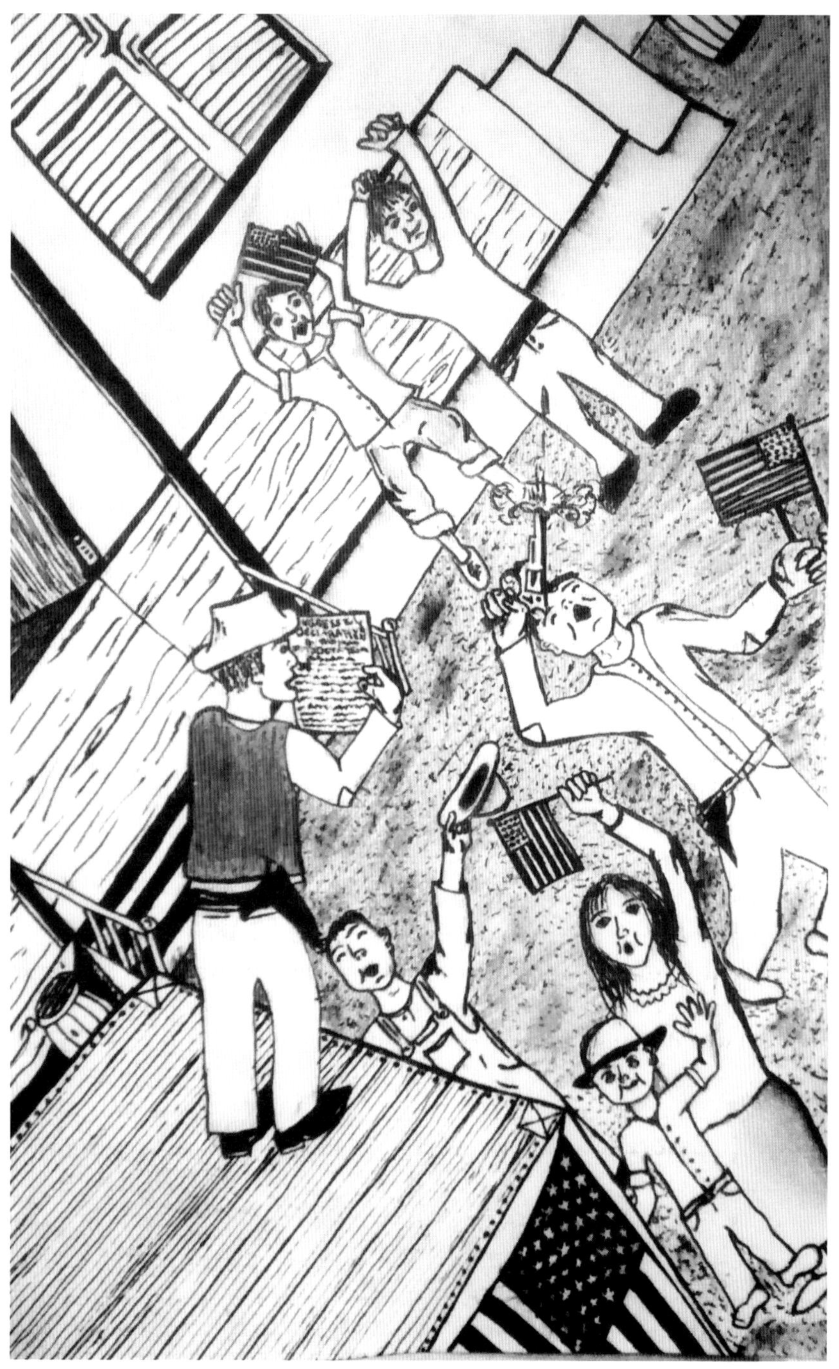

Fourth of July celebration. *Drawing by Angie Hopkins.*

Miners saw the necessity of law enforcement when they began to argue over claims. Miners' Courts were set up within the districts, and a decision by the Miners' Court was final and immediate. Richard Sopris served as president of the Miners' Union and helped establish laws relating to mining claims. Then he was involved in maintenance of law and order.

The Fourth of July 1859 found Sopris back in Denver. The first celebration of Independence Day was held in a grove on the Platte River. The festivities included reading the Declaration of Independence to a patriotic crowd, which was performed by Captain Richard Sopris. According to the *Rocky Mountain News*, "Every man in the crowd had a formidable looking pistol and they gave vent to their enthusiasm by firing volleys into the air. When one of the speakers made a telling point, the women would clap their hands and the men kept up the shooting."

The area that would become Colorado was still outside the United States. The 1854 Kansas-Nebraska Act had created the territories of Kansas and Nebraska with the dividing line on the fortieth parallel. A look at a map shows the fortieth parallel on a line from east to west just north of Denver. So Denver and the surrounding areas were in Kansas Territory.

The capital of Kansas Territory was Leavenworth, seven hundred miles from the remote mines in its western reaches. The westernmost section of the territory was declared a county, named after one of the local Indian tribes: the Arapahoe. As the population grew, the miners began to see the need for representation in the nation's capital. They were largely ignored by the Kansas Territorial Legislature, but in 1859 they were told to elect a representative for Arapahoe County.

Those interested in separate statehood went on a different path. Delegates were elected to draft a constitution, and an election was held to approve the constitution on the first Monday in September 1859. The proposal for statehood was defeated. Having suspected that there were not enough votes

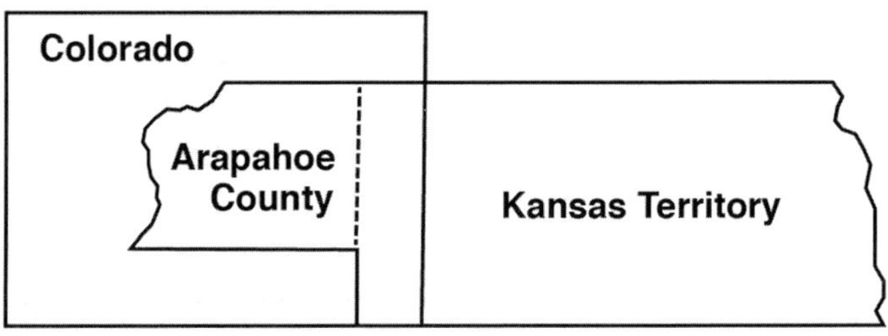

Arapahoe County map. *Drawing by author.*

to pass the statehood issue, delegates to the convention were ready to propose that another election be immediately scheduled.

This election was held on the first Monday in October. Two issues were on the ballot: selection of a delegate to the U.S. Congress to propose authorization of a separate territory—Jefferson Territory—and election of delegates to form a Provisional Territorial Government.

Both issues were passed: Beverly D. Williams was elected as the delegate to the U.S. Congress and a Provisional Government of the Territory of Jefferson was created, complete with all the requisite elected officials. R.W. Steele was the first governor. Richard Sopris, H.P. Bennet and A.C. Hunt worked together to establish the framework of what they referred to as the "People's Government." The provisional government held its first session on November 7, 1859, in Denver City. A constitution was framed and adopted. The territory was divided into legislative districts. Civil and criminal codes were enacted.

Williams was not successful in promoting Jefferson Territory to the U.S. Congress—with the threat of a war looming, there was little interest in discussing a new territory in the West.

Meanwhile, Arapahoe County was legally part of Kansas Territory, and the Kansas Territorial Legislature had directed the county to elect a

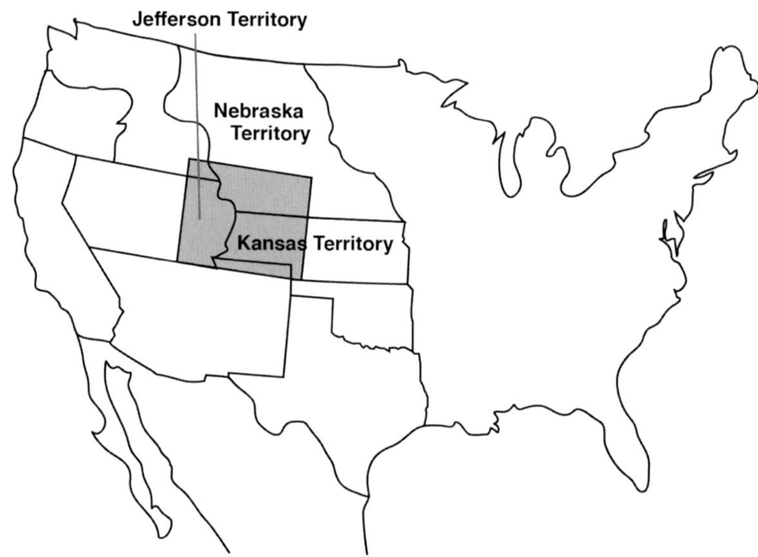

Jefferson Territory map. *Drawing by author.*

representative. At a separate election in November 1859, Captain Richard Sopris was the winning choice.

Sopris dutifully went to Kansas to serve his term as the Arapahoe County representative. One accomplishment that was to have long-lasting effects was the Kansas Territorial Legislature's approval of the incorporation of the Capitol Hydraulic Company of Arapahoe County. Sopris was one of the designated owners of the company that was to issue capital stock for its undertakings. Section 2 of the incorporating legislation read:

> *Said company shall have the power and exclusive right to direct the water from the bed of the South Platte River at any point they may select between the Platte Cañon and the mouth of Cherry Creek, and also to direct the water from the bed of Cherry Creek at any point within six miles of its mouth, and to conduct the water from both said streams by canal or ditch across the plains or intervening lands to the cities of Auraria, Denver and Highland, in the County of Arapahoe, Territory of Kansas, and have the exclusive privilege of using and controlling the same for mechanical, agricultural, mining and city purposes.*

Approved on February 21, 1860, this charter was not only the authorization to build the Denver City Ditch but the foundation for water rights that are still adjudicated in the water courts. Sopris explained, "Nobody can take water out of the Platte River as long as the City wants it."

Water rights laws go back in history to when man first began to grow crops. Historically, Riparian Water Rights gave the owner of property adjacent to the water supply preferential rights. In areas that are arid or semi-arid, an alternate doctrine has developed that "first in time, first in right" is the factor deciding whose water rights have greater priority. The initial premise is that the first one to make beneficial use of the water has the better right. Accompanying premises, however, are that water should not be wasted or used excessively, and water may not be used in a manner that detrimentally affects others. This system of water rights has led to numerous court cases all through the years.

Sopris was also able to get the Kansas legislature to approve charters for roads in the mountains, insurance companies, banking companies and telegraph companies. But one of the critical things that Sopris was entrusted to do was convince Kansas lawmakers not to include Arapahoe County in their state, as Kansas was actively lobbying Congress for statehood.

A second session of the Jefferson Territory Provisional Government was convened on January 23, 1860. In April, an official act of the legislature consolidated Auraria and Denver into a single municipality. The Denver name prevailed, and Auraria became known as West Denver.

The first mayor of Denver was John C. Moore. While serving his term as mayor, Moore began publishing the second newspaper in Denver, *The Denver Mountaineer*. Moore had strong Southern sympathies and sold the newspaper early in 1861 as he left to join the Confederate Army.

The Jefferson Territorial Legislature paralleled acts and decisions that were made in the Kansas Territorial Legislature. The difference was since Congress had not approved it, Jefferson Territory was not a legal entity.

And there was no agreement with the resident Indians, who became increasingly concerned about white people invading what they still considered their land.

4
Mount Sopris

As Richard Sopris finished his term at the Kansas Territorial Legislature, he decided that it was time to bring his family from Indiana to his newly adopted home. He went back to Indiana and made arrangements for all of them to pack up their belongings for a permanent move. They traveled by train as far as Quincy, Missouri, then boarded a riverboat that took them downriver twenty miles to Hannibal. From there, it was a short ride on the rails to St. Joseph and another boat ride to Atchison, Kansas. There, they awaited the shipment of their belongings. Sopris had purchased a wagon and horses, an ambulance pulled by mules and a ten- by ten-foot tent for their journey across the plains. They packed a generous stock of provisions that included hams, bacon, flour, hard bread, sugar, coffee, tea, rice, beans, homing cheese, pickles, sardines, lobsters, canned fruits, vinegar, molasses and spices of all kinds. They purchased fresh eggs and milk from farmers along the way.

Indiana Sopris was the oldest daughter of the Sopris family. She was almost twenty-one years old when the family set out across the Kansas prairies in their wagon. She kept a journal, making daily entries for the month it took them to arrive in Denver. The oldest sibling was her brother Allen, then twenty-two years old, and the youngest was George, then only seven years old.

Indiana and her younger sister Irene were popular among the young men they happened to meet, and their evenings at the nightly campfire were spent singing and storytelling. Indiana wrote in her journal of the Indians

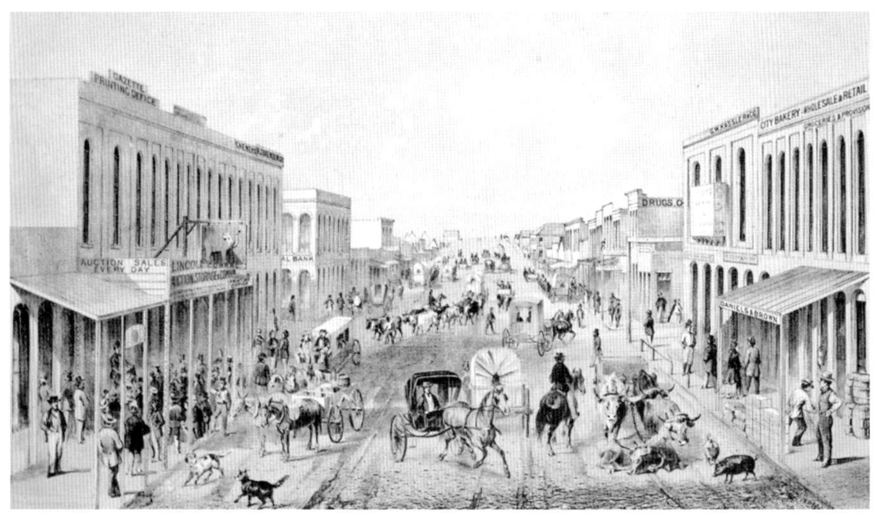

Blake Street, Denver, Colorado. *From* Sketches of Colorado: Its Cities, Principal Towns and Mountain Scenery, *New York, A.E. Mathews, 1866.*

they saw on their way; she admired the young children and offered food to the adults. All those the Sopris family met were friendly.

The route they followed took them to Kearney, in Nebraska Territory, and they followed the Platte River from there. The last entry in Indiana's journal was dated April 23, 1860. A few days later, the Sopris family arrived at their new home in Denver.

The town in the early 1860s was described by Susan Ashley, wife of Eli Ashley, who was chief clerk of the Surveyor General's Office under the first governor, William Gilpin. According to Susan, West Denver, formerly Auraria, had the greater number of residences. It had wells of good water and possibilities of trees, gardens and flowers. East Denver had the greater number of businesses. It was on higher ground but much dryer, with no prospect of growing anything more beautiful than cactus.

East Denver's streets were occupied by corrals; hay, grain and sales stables; wholesale supply stores; commission houses; and a plethora of boarding houses, saloons and gambling places. Although West Denver was primarily residential, there were also a few supply stores, a planing mill, an iron foundry, a jail and a large commission house. The wholesale storage and commission house was owned by J.B. Doyle, one of the leading freighters on the old Santa Fe Trail. Located on the corner of Ferry (11th) and Larimer Streets, the two-story building was converted into a hotel: the Lindell Hotel. Richard Sopris rented the building for his family's use.

Susan knew the Sopris family and described the two daughters, Indiana and Irene, as "much sought young ladies." She also described the Indians who roamed the streets of Denver in those days. They were all apparently quite friendly, to the point of entering homes unannounced when the doors were unlocked. When they were asked to leave by the firm command "puck-a-chee," they would reluctantly go outside but line up at the windows and peek in.

Sopris had barely settled his family in Denver when he took his oldest son, Allen, with him on his newest adventure. In July 1860, they joined a group of people who thought that most of the readily accessible gold in central Colorado had been found and made plans to explore the possibilities of gold deposits farther west.

Although they declared that the purpose of the expedition was to locate new minerals, more than just miners accompanied the party. The night before the party left, Captain Sopris was elected the leader. Two guides were identified, and a recording secretary was appointed. The entourage also included a doctor, a botanist and an artist/surveyor. "Each man was well mounted and fully armed, and the party carried all the tools necessary to build boats or gold sluices," according to Sopris' later account.

The job of the recording secretary was to send frequent articles back to the *Rocky Mountain News* telling of their findings. In his first installment to the newspaper, D.C. Collier explained that the object of the group was to "explore as far as practicable the southern tributaries of Grand River, and the country lying between the Grand and the Green." The Grand River later became known as the Colorado River.

Early in July they set out, traveling through South Park toward the Blue River near Breckenridge. Captain Sopris rode a mule that had been named Jerry. Mules, noted for their stubbornness as well as their reliability and surefootedness, were personified in Jerry. One day, Sopris rode Jerry up the side of a mountain, hoping to get a better view of the land his group was headed toward. Jerry sank into a snowbank, where he remained stuck in spite of the captain's efforts to get him out. The mule had evidently decided that his day's work was done and refused to make any effort on his own behalf.

After a number of attempts to extract the mule, Sopris equated him to the biblical Baalam's ass—whose stubbornness has been noted in that holy book—whacked him a few times for encouragement and finally left the creature in the snowbank. Painstakingly descending the mountainside, Sopris explained his solo appearance at camp and told his fellow explorers that the mule was a lost cause.

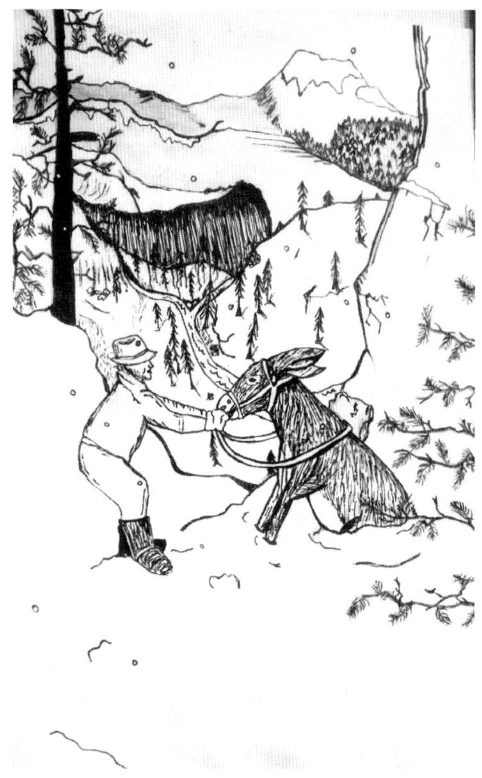

Jerry stuck in the snowbank. *Drawing by Angie Hopkins.*

Charles Marion, the surveyor, said in disbelief, "I can't get along without Jerry." Captain Sopris, no doubt still peeved at the mule's behavior, replied, "YOU can't get along without him? He's my mule, not yours." The surveyor explained that he had learned to gauge the distance covered every day by the amount of time the mule took to cover a mile. At the end of each day, Marion would calculate the amount of distance covered using Jerry's gait and the amount of time spent on the trail. This methodology proved later to be surprisingly accurate.

The next morning, several members of the party went up the mountainside to where Jerry was stuck and retrieved him. Jerry evidently had decided that he was up for a new day's work, and besides, he was hungry for fodder.

Reaching the Grand River at its confluence with what would later be named the Roaring Fork River, the explorers stopped to camp. They discovered hot springs and proceeded to wash their clothing. The clothes came out dirtier looking than they were before the wash. Captain Sopris told them to look for a soda spring instead of the iron spring they had been using. Upon the second washing, the clothes took on a cleaner look.

The Green River was located to the northwest of the Grand, so the group would have to cross the Grand in order to proceed. After an unsuccessful attempt with a raft, the tools were brought out to fell a fir tree and build an actual boat. This took some time, and while the boat was under construction, Captain Sopris found a large tree on which he carved, "These springs were discovered on July 23, 1860, by Captain Sopris and a party of prospectors."

The next day, the boat, dubbed the *Western Wanderer*, was loaded with provisions and camp equipment and launched, crossing the Grand River safely. Getting the animals across proved to be a bit more difficult, but they were loaded two at a time on the boat and ferried to the other side.

While the explorers worked on their crossing, they looked south toward a scenic mountain that was later measured at 12,823 feet above sea level. They began to call it the Cap'n Sopris Mountain, and it later was officially named Mount Sopris. Thirty-one years later, Captain Sopris would return to the site, now the prosperous town of Glenwood Springs. He would stay in the Hotel Glenwood and relate to newspaper reporters how he and his group of explorers had first found the site. Local historians noted that, while the explorers were there, Sopris had become ill. Ute Indians in the area advised them to take him to the healing hot springs for a cure.

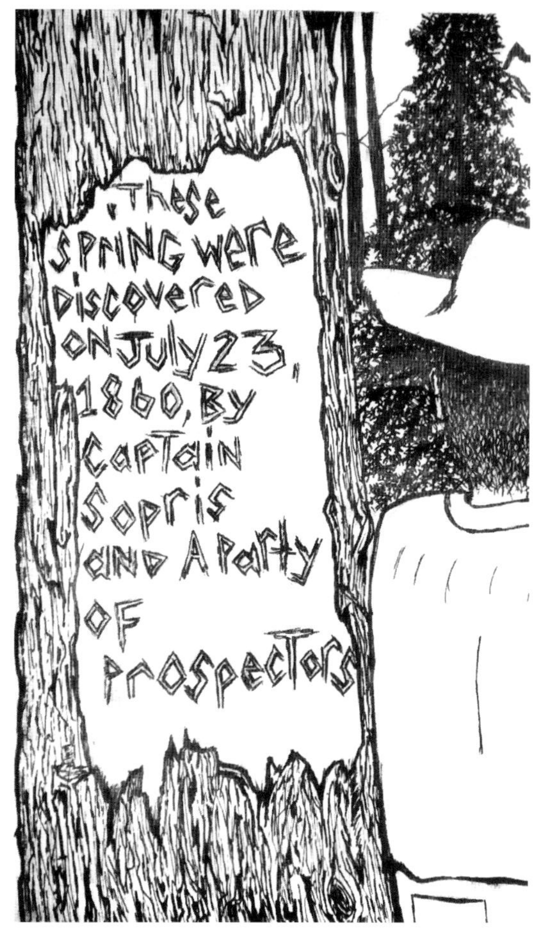

Glenwood Springs, discovered by the Sopris party. *Drawing by Angie Hopkins.*

It was there, according to Sopris, that he met and talked to Chief Colorow and obtained his permission to pass through the territory.

After crossing the Grand River, the group camped that night on the other side. They sank the *Western Wanderer* where they could find it on their way back. The group went as far as the junction of the White and Green Rivers, located in what is now the state of Utah. Having found no evidence that there were large deposits of gold in the area, the party split up. Part of them, including Captain Sopris, turned back toward the east, toward home, and the rest, including Allen Sopris, Dr. Arnold and

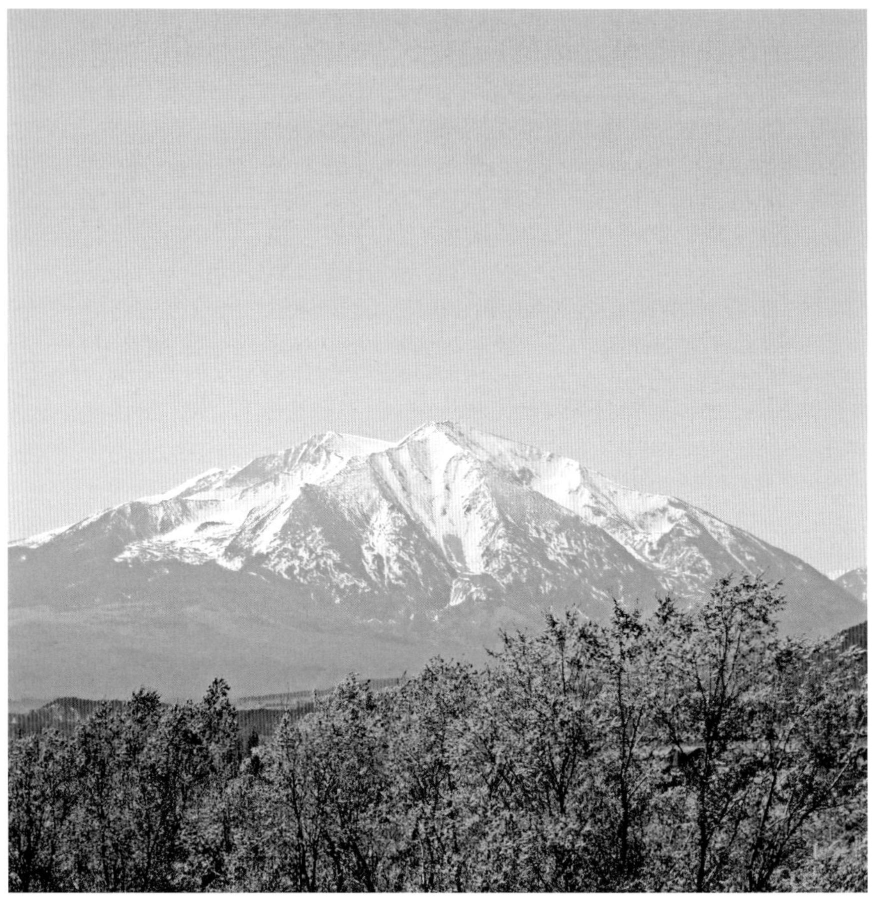

Mount Sopris. *Photo by Christie Wright.*

Collier, the secretary who was sending accounts of the trip to the *Rocky Mountain News*, went south.

The men in the latter group eventually found themselves near the Rio Grande and, having used up nearly all their supplies, headed east toward Fort Garland. Part of the entourage, including Collier, obtained some of the few supplies available at the fort and headed north. They found the waters of the Arkansas River and crossed over Poncha Pass on their way to California Gulch and on to Denver. In his submissions to the *Rocky Mountain News*, Collier described the geological formations, various plants they found and the general terrain they passed through. He noted the discovery of a native pie plant that turned out to be a delicious food item. He was describing a rhubarb plant. Collier was quite sure of the presence of diamonds in the area based on his observations.

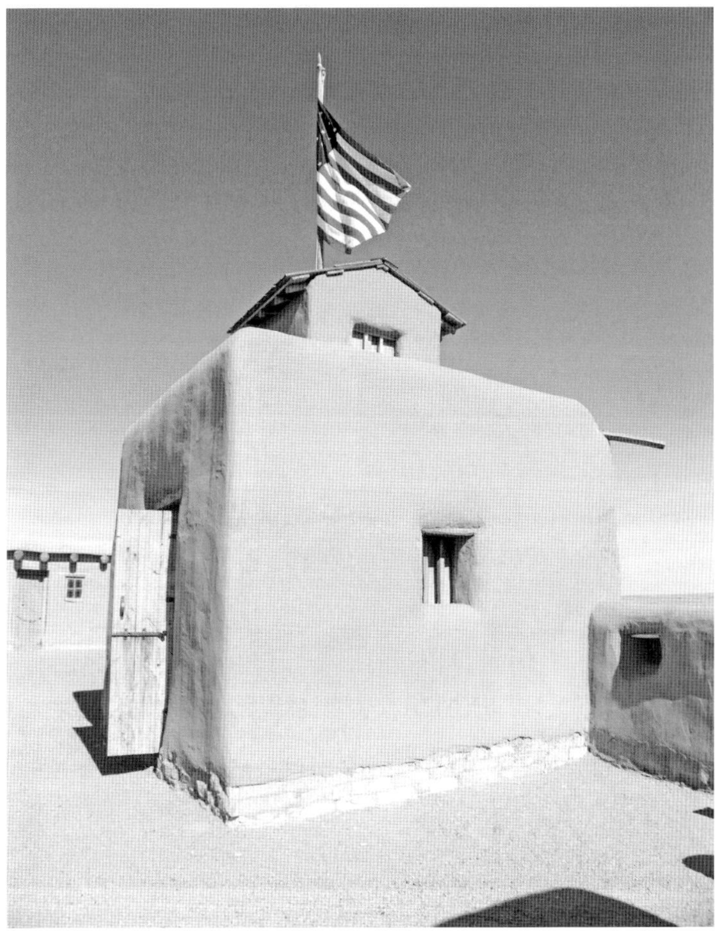

Parapet at Fort Garland. *Photo by author.*

On October 24, Allen Sopris sent a letter to his father from Fort Garland announcing the party's safe arrival there. In his letter, Allen announced his intent to join another party that was headed to the San Juan Mines, part of the loosely knit Baker Expedition.

Although the Sopris prospectors were somewhat disappointed about the lack of gold, the information they recorded along the way proved to be an invaluable resource for mapmakers trying to chart the geographic features of what would become Colorado. Under the direction of first Territorial Governor William Gilpin, Ebert's *1865 Map of Colorado Territory, Embracing the Central Gold Region* was drawn, using much of the information provided by the Sopris party.

5
Bummers

While Captain Sopris and his group had been exploring the mountains and river valleys to the west, the town of Denver was experiencing a wave of violence and crime. Although many were law-abiding citizens, a certain element had respect for neither the faraway Kansas Territory laws nor the illegitimate Jefferson Territory attempt at establishing a lawful environment.

Early in 1860, a number of idlers and drifters came to town. They frequented the local liquor establishments and routinely robbed and stole for a living. They were proud of the name they called themselves: "Bummers."

A ranchman had brought a wagonload of wild turkeys into Auraria to sell to a public eager for fresh meat. While he was negotiating the sale, several of the Bummers made off with his wagon and all of the cargo. A neighboring businessman, William Middaugh, saw the theft and identified the culprits to the city marshal. By this time, the local citizens were fed up with the brazen thievery and appointed a committee to investigate the crime.

Now identified by name, the thieves, emboldened by large quantities of liquor, made threats and boasts about what they would do to anybody who tried to apprehend them. One tried to make good on his threats as he accosted the marshal on the street with a bowie knife. The marshal simply clouted the Bummer with the butt of his rifle and left him unconscious on the street.

Another of the Bummers got the drop on the marshal and poked his sixshooter into the lawman's stomach, loudly cursing and threatening. He

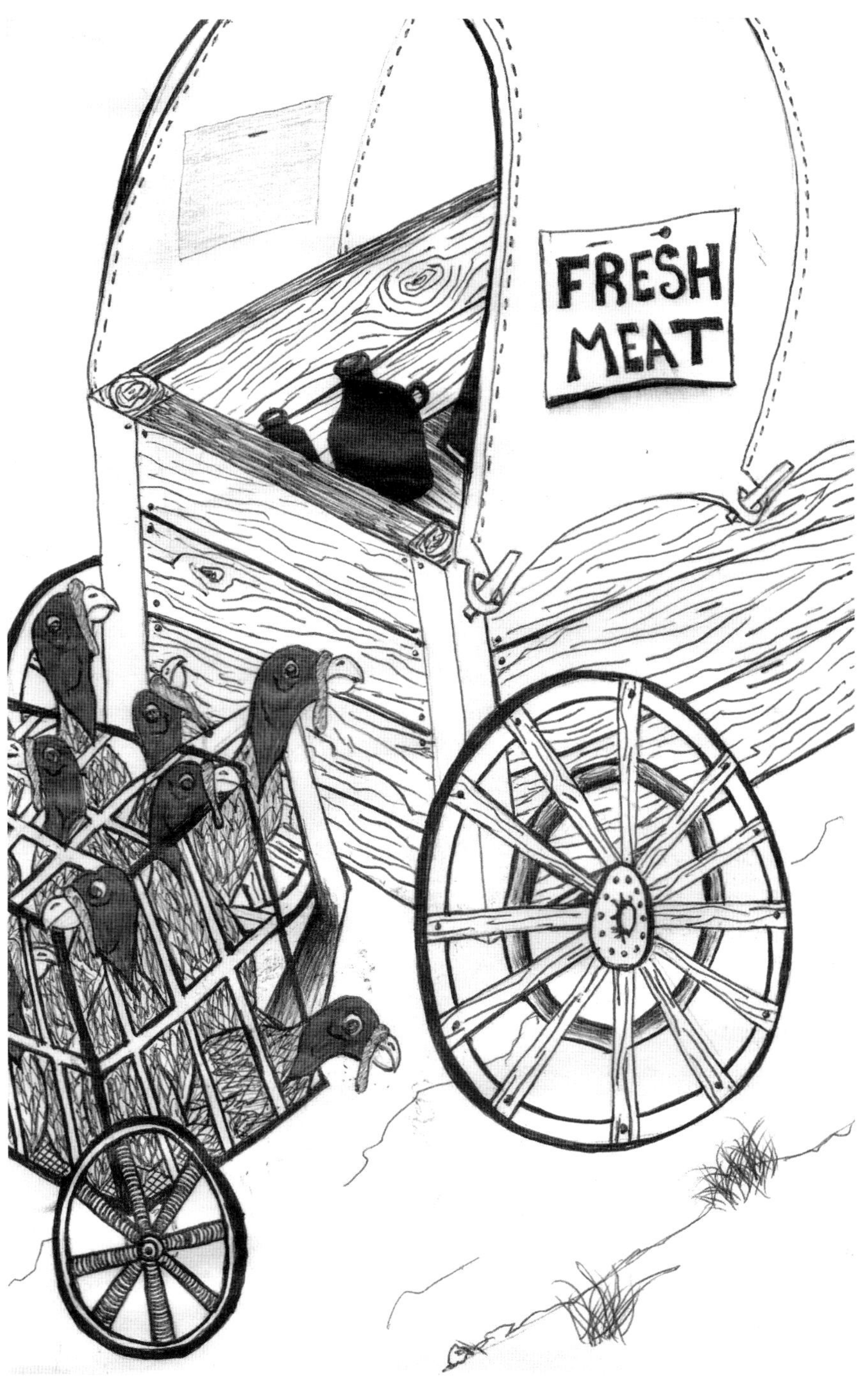

Turkey War. *Drawing by Angie Hopkins.*

was, however, just sober enough to recognize the distinctive *click*, *click*, *click* of several guns being cocked and aimed at him, so he turned and fled.

The Bummer who had been clouted with the marshal's rifle revived and turned his anger toward Middaugh, who had identified him. He waited outside the Vasquez House, a hotel where Middaugh routinely stopped for supper. As Middaugh opened the door to leave, the Bummer fired a shot at him at point-blank range. By this time, the would-be assassin was so angry and liquored up beyond reason that he missed his target. Several of Middaugh's friends accompanied him toward his home, but another grossly inebriated Bummer fired a shot out of the second-story window of the hotel. This, too, missed.

The next day, the citizens' hearing was held. The judge listened to the report by the investigating committee, to which had been added the unprovoked assaults on Middaugh. After interviewing witnesses, the judge proclaimed that the People's Court had resolved that the four Bummers involved in the incident were to be given five hours to leave town permanently. If they for any reason were found after that time, they would be summarily hanged.

The "Jefferson Rangers" had recently been formed as a local militia to enforce the peace. They patrolled the town for several days to make sure that the banished Bummers did not return. This ended the incident that came to be known as the "Turkey War." But it did not end the violence that permeated the town.

Toward the end of July, local businessmen formed a Vigilance Committee that met frequently to serve immediate justice on murderers. There was a temporary lull in violent crimes, which caused some of the local attorneys to announce in the *Rocky Mountain Herald* that they were closing their offices due to lack of business.

The relative peace came to a halt as several of the local ranchers began to experience thefts of their horses, mules and oxen in large numbers. The men on the Vigilance Committee vigorously tried to find out who was behind the thefts, but the outlaws evaded them. Finally, they got a break. An old French trapper had camped along the Platte, where he found and recognized the tracks of one of his own mounts that had been stolen. He had been following the tracks for three days when he sited the smoke of a camp. Waiting until dark, he crept close enough to look. What he saw was a large number of horses and a few men, one of whom he recognized as an outlaw known as Black Hawk.

Knowing he could not approach them alone, the trapper came back to town to report what he had seen. Meanwhile, Black Hawk decided to come

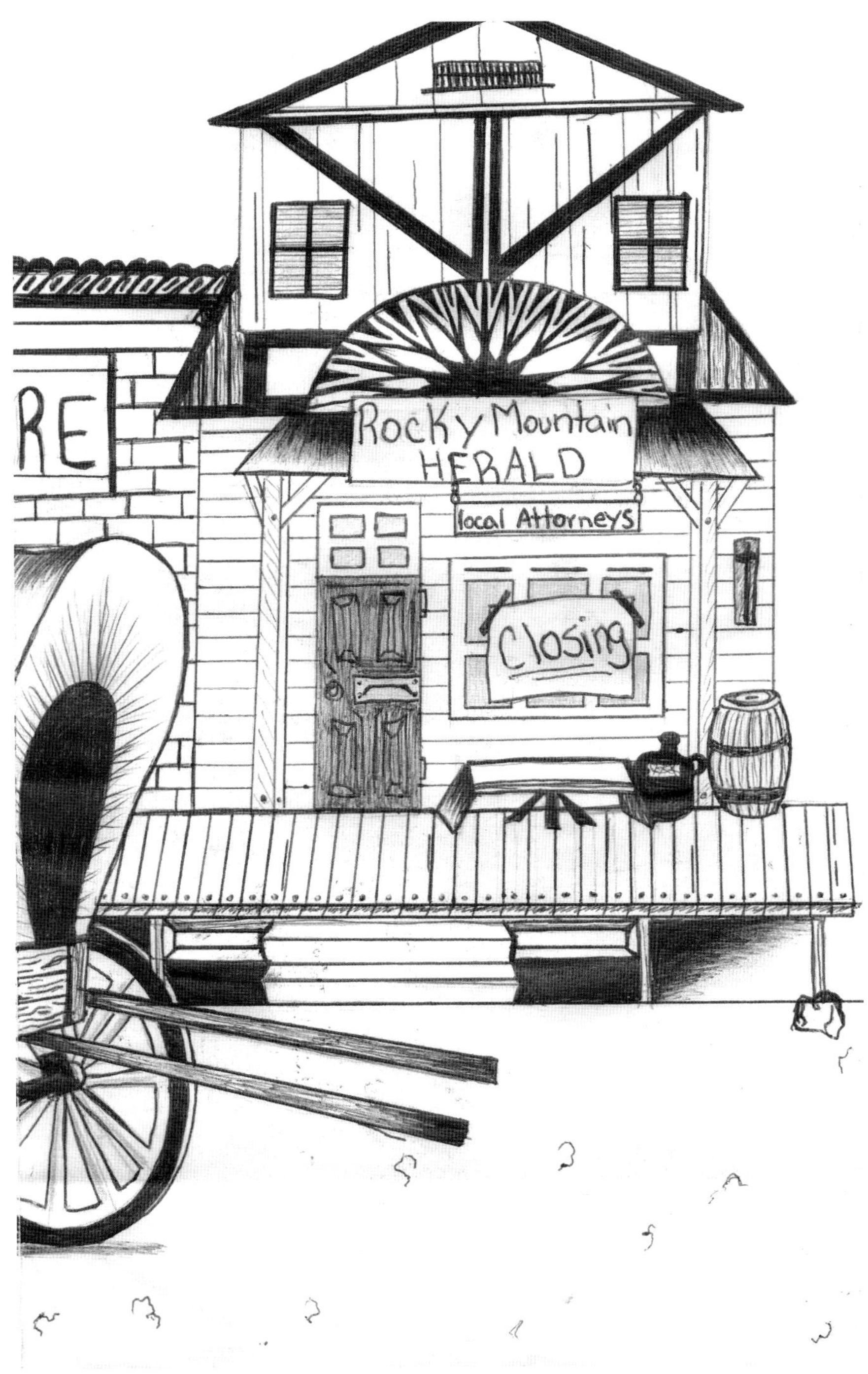

Attorney notice. *Drawing by Angie Hopkins.*

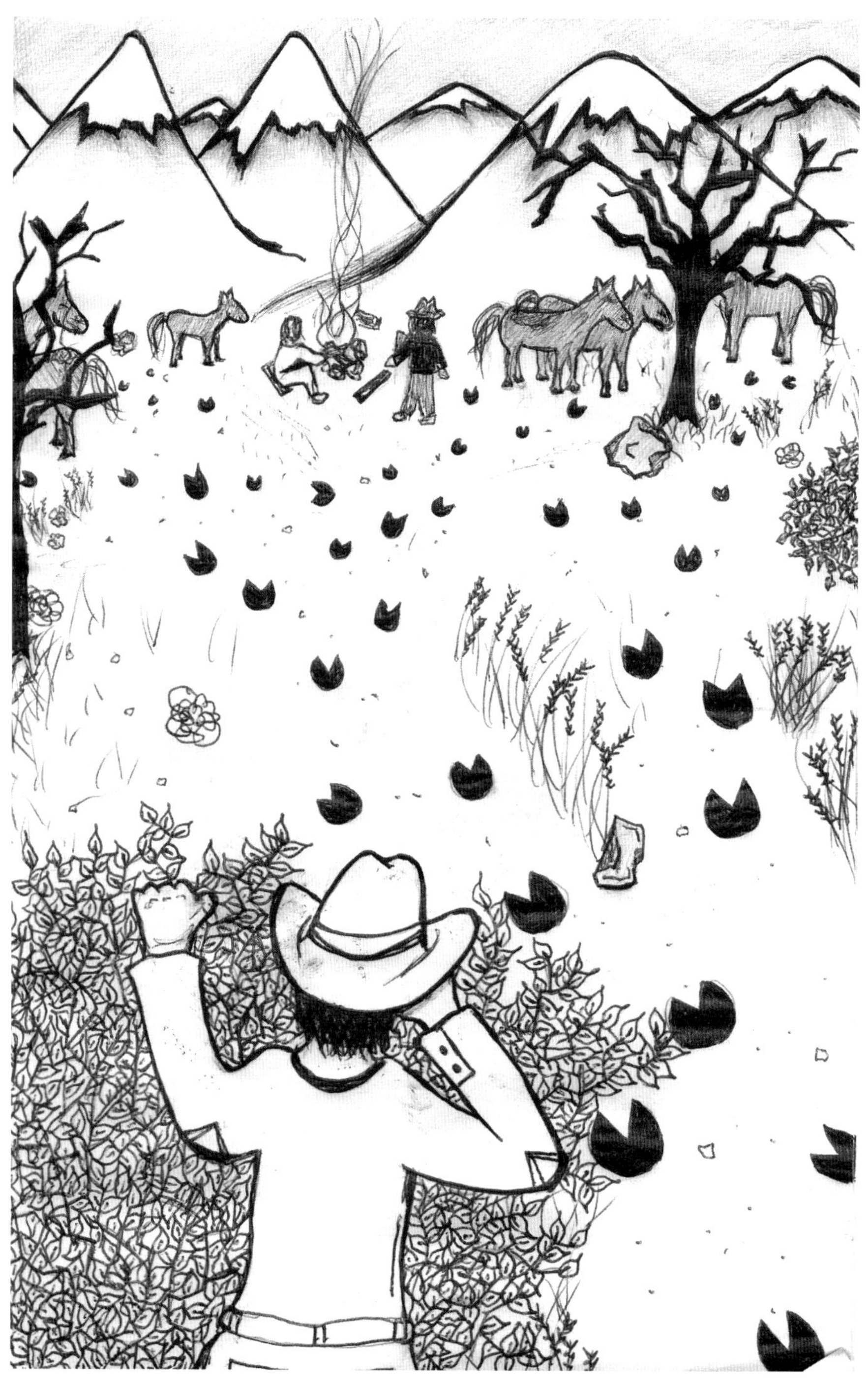

Campsite of Thieves. *Drawing by Angie Hopkins.*

into town for supplies. Not knowing that he had been spotted and identified, he was surprised when some of the vigilantes intercepted him a few miles from town. He could not explain the stolen horses in his possession. The vigilantes brought him to town and locked him up. They made an agreement with him that if he wrote out a confession and identified the leaders of his gang, they would escort him out of town with a simple banishment.

But the news of his capture leaked out, and that night, a lynch party broke into the cellar room where he was confined. The lynch mob apparently did not notice his partially completed confession as they dragged him out and hanged him from a cottonwood tree near Cherry Creek. The Vigilance Committee did find the confession with several names on it. They had also learned from Black Hawk that he was part of an organization of horse thieves that was divided into districts, with a leader for each district. The stock that was stolen was passed through the districts until they could be safely sold.

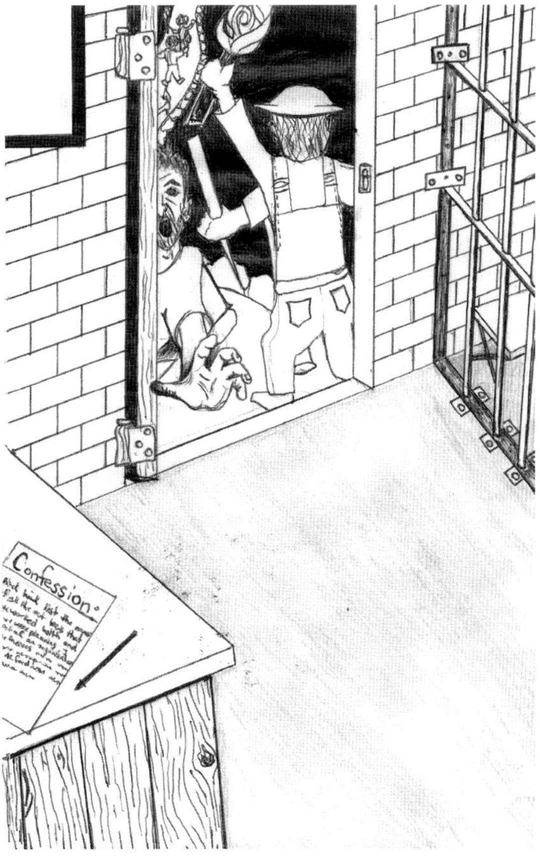

Confession. *Drawing by Angie Hopkins.*

The outlaw had specifically named A.C. Ford as the one in charge of the local district. Ford was a local attorney who had successfully defended a number of those accused of crimes but who otherwise was known as a prominent citizen. When Ford heard that Black Hawk had been executed, he decided it was time to leave. He got on a stagecoach that was headed east to Council Bluffs, Iowa, where his wife lived.

Richard Sopris, familiar with the activities of the Vigilance Committee, described what happened. The vigilantes planned to stop the stage several miles out of town and apprehend

Ford. As they took him out of the stagecoach, they told the driver to go ahead without the passenger. Ford recognized the men as members of the Vigilance Committee and, knowing his fate, asked that he be shot rather than hanged. The vigilantes complied with his request and left his body, along with $300 or $400 in gold, a gold watch and a finger ring.

One of the men went back and took the valuables, but he was found out and made to return the watch and ring (he had already spent the money), which were sent to Ford's wife.

Another incident in December of that year involved Captain Sopris. Thomas Freeman worked a small ranch a short distance north of town. He raised vegetables and, in the winter, bought hay and brought it into Denver to sell. His disappearance was noticed when he didn't bring his usual load of hay into town. It was known that he had last been seen with Patrick Waters, a known Bummer, as they set out in Freeman's wagon to purchase hay.

Then a train of freight wagons traveling along the Platte River discovered a blood-stained wagon that had been backed over a cliff. The day before, one of the hands with the train had noticed a man riding an unsaddled mount and leading a blind horse.

Knowing that Waters had been with Freeman, the Vigilance Committee decided it should look for him. They acted on another clue that had come to them from a traveler who had decided to stop in the same bar where they were meeting. The traveler described a man he had seen with a description that fit Patrick Waters. The committee immediately went to the location the traveler described and found Waters asleep. He was wearing Freeman's hat and boots but claimed they had been given to him.

Members of the committee took Waters with them as they returned to the location where the bloodied wagon had been found. They searched the area but found nothing more. Then they lost patience. They threatened to hang Waters on the spot if he didn't tell them what he knew. They went so far as to tie his hands behind his back and strap his feet together. Waters didn't react until they put a noose around his neck. At that point, he broke down and confessed. He led the vigilantes to the spot where he had dumped the body in a thicket of willows.

The vigilantes brought Freeman's remains and Waters back to Denver. Richard Sopris, who was a fellow Mason with a number of the Vigilance Committee members, was appointed the administrator of Freeman's estate.

Waters finally confessed that he had been hired by Freeman for one dollar a day to help him with his hay-buying trip. On the way, they got into an argument, and Waters decided to kill his companion and rob him. He picked up the tailgate of the wagon and hit Freeman with it. That merely knocked Freeman unconscious. Then Waters loaded a shotgun, jammed it into the back of Freeman's neck and fired. He emptied Freeman's pockets and removed some of his clothing, then dumped the body in the bushes. He drove back along the road for several miles, unhitched the team and pushed the wagon over a bluff. He mounted one horse and led the blind one, heading east.

Waters was tried by the People's Court and found guilty of murder. On December 21, he was escorted to the gallows, having been given two days to settle his affairs. His hanging was the last execution performed by the People's Court.

6

Glorieta Pass

Early in November 1860, a resolution of the Denver City Council authorized an election to levy a tax of $3,000 for the purpose of building a jail and city hall. Richard Sopris was one of the presiding election judges in West Denver (formerly Auraria). A few weeks later, the "For Tax" or "Against Tax" election was indefinitely postponed.

In a more far-reaching election that same month, Abraham Lincoln was elected president of the United States. This accelerated the push for secession of Southern states, as well as the clamor of the western territories to be recognized.

In January 1861, Kansas became a state with its present western boundary, leaving Arapahoe County out. A bill to create Colorado Territory was introduced in Congress, passed on February 28 and signed by James Buchanan, one of the final acts of his presidency.

As soon as Lincoln took office, events rapidly propelled the nation into a civil war. Southern canons fired on Fort Sumter on April 12, making the hostilities official. Lincoln appointed William Gilpin, an avowed Unionist, as the first governor of the fledgling Colorado Territory. Gilpin arrived in Denver on May 29 ready to take charge. He was no stranger to the territory, as he had been in Fremont's entourage in 1843 when they traveled through the territory on their way west.

William Gilpin was born on October 4, 1813, near Philadelphia, Pennsylvania. His wealthy Quaker family sent him to the University of Pennsylvania, from which he graduated in 1833. He went on to West Point and completed that program in 1836. He spent time in the United States Army before he joined John Charles Fremont in 1843 to explore the West. He again joined the military to be part of the Mexican-American War in 1848. Although he alternated a law practice with writing, he developed a futurist philosophy about civilization, commerce and wealth in which the American West was prominent.

The year 1860 found him writing a book called *The Central Gold Region*, in which he described the mountains, seas and mineral deposits of the earth and concluded that "one radical fact is discernible to everybody. The amount of gold and silver coin among any people is the gauge of their civilization."

Immediately upon his arrival in the Colorado Territory, Gilpin began to establish the framework of a government. Seventeen counties were immediately carved out of the territory. Gilpin assessed the military capability, which then consisted of two garrison forts: Fort Garland in the San Luis Valley and Fort Wise, soon renamed Fort Lyon, on the Arkansas River.

Local law enforcement had been entrusted to two local militia groups, the Jefferson Rangers, who were active during the infamous Turkey War, and the Denver Guards, whose commander was an avowed Southern sympathizer. Both militia groups had been disbanded during the winter of 1860.

Governor Gilpin organized a military staff, appointing an adjutant general, a paymaster, a quartermaster general and a purchasing agent. A Denver attorney, John Slough, was commissioned from Washington, D.C., to recruit two companies of infantry to relieve the regulars at Fort Garland, who could then be sent east to support the Union cause.

Gilpin announced his intent to recruit and organize a full regiment of Colorado volunteers. He appointed Colonel John Slough to command and Lieutenant Colonel Samuel Tappan next in command.

In addition to a vigorous enlistment campaign, Governor Gilpin sent out his purchasing agent to acquire any weapons and ammunition he could find. He discovered that the few Confederates left in the area were also out purchasing weapons and took steps to discourage them.

Another military figure was offered the position of chaplain, as he was the presiding elder of the Methodist Episcopal Church in the Rocky Mountain District. But John Chivington insisted instead on being assigned a fighting position and was awarded the rank of major.

Captains were appointed and assigned the task of recruiting for their companies that would make up the First Regiment of Colorado Volunteers. They were: Company A, Captain Edward Wynkoop; Company B, Captain Samuel Logan; Company C, Captain Richard Sopris; Company D,

Captain Jacob Downing; Company E, Captain Scott Anthony; Company F, Captain Samuel Cook; Company G, Captain Josiah Hambleton; Company H, Captain George Sanborn; Company I, Captain Charles Mailie; and Company K, Captain Charles Marion.

Recruitment quotas were met by September, and a barracks was constructed two and a half miles north of the mouth of Cherry Creek. It was named Camp Weld after first Territorial Secretary Lewis Ledyard Weld.

The enclosure embraced about thirty acres. The buildings consisted of officers' headquarters, quarters for soldiers, mess rooms, a guard house, et cetera. A building designated as soldiers' quarters could accommodate twenty-five men and consisted of a mess room, fireplaces at either end of the building and sleeping compartments.

While the Federal government had appointed a governor for the new Colorado Territory and approved the establishment of military companies in the new territory, it had neglected to approve a budget for any of the essential activities. Organizing and building a military force entails not only the expense of constructing their quarters but the expense of providing them arms, clothing, food and supplies as well. And the cost mounts up quickly.

Despite the lack of official permission from Congress, Governor Gilpin began to issue promissory drafts on the Federal government for these necessary items. When requests for payment reached Washington, D.C., and were refused, the local merchants were incensed. The aggregate amount of the drafts issued by Gilpin amounted to $375,000. Even though Colorado's first territorial governor made a trip to the nation's capital to explain and request payment of the drafts, he was rebuffed. Some of the drafts were eventually paid, but it took years, and many of the merchants were never paid.

As soldiers came down from the mountains to join their compatriots, they filled up Camp Weld. Although they participated in training exercises and other camp duties, they were left with a lot of time on their hands, which they, as young men do, filled with frequenting the local saloons. Since there was no money available to pay them, they took to extracting items from merchants and local residents. Complaints were made and articles written in the local newspaper about "Disorderly Soldiers."

Meanwhile, Confederate President Jefferson Davis had appointed General Henry Hopkins Sibley to raise three regiments of Southern troops in West Texas. The Confederate plan was to march up the Rio Grande, take Santa Fe, capture Fort Union in New Mexico for its stores, exploit the Colorado gold fields and head west to take California. The long-range plan was to establish ports on the Pacific Coast and eventually invade Mexico.

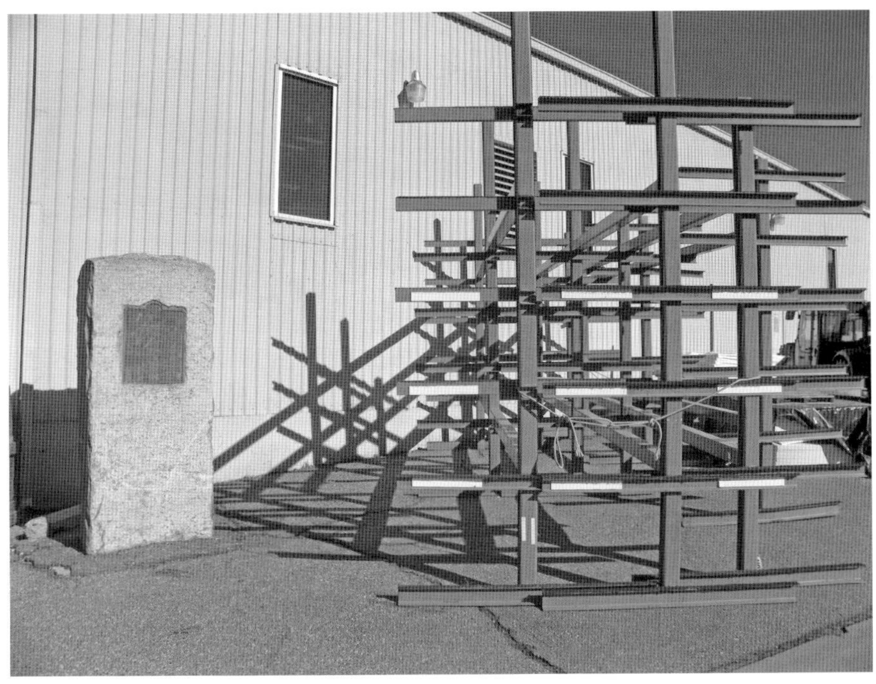

Above: Camp Weld marker. *Photo by author.*

Right: Close up of Camp Weld marker. *Photo by author.*

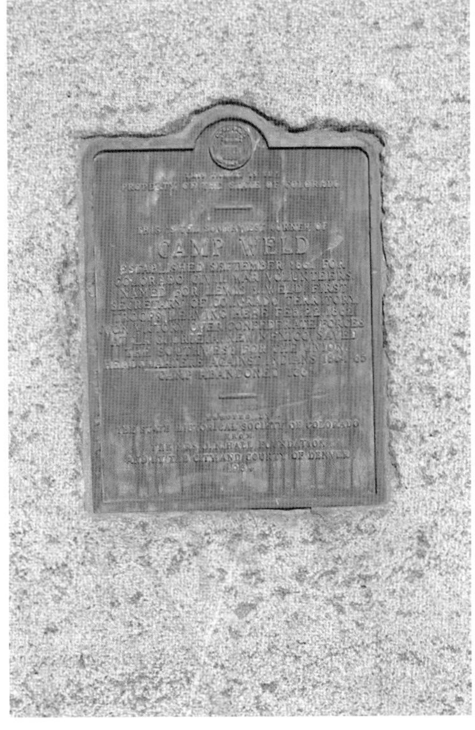

Texas seceded from the Union in March 1861. General Sibley took over the military forts in that state. During President Buchanan's term of office, his secretary of war had fortuitously stocked Fort Union in New Mexico with provisions. As Southern states seceded, Southern sympathizers resigned from Union posts and joined the Confederate cause. Two of the forts in New Mexico were still under Union control: Fort Craig, along the Rio Grande, and Fort Union, northeast of Santa Fe.

Edward Canby was appointed Union commander of the Department of New Mexico and established headquarters at Fort Craig. When General Canby got word that Sibley was on his way north, Canby appealed to Governor Gilpin for two companies of militia to reinforce his troops at Fort Craig. Colorado Territory answered by sending two companies that had been recruited in Canon City in addition to those recruited and housed at Camp Weld. Ford's Company and Dodd's Company made up the Second Colorado Volunteer Infantry. Ford took his company to Fort Craig to join General Canby, and Dodd took his to Fort Union.

General Canby again got word that Sibley was on the move and headed up the Rio Grande valley. Canby requested more reinforcements from Colorado Territory. The troops at Camp Weld, who had spent the previous several months at leisure, suddenly had a job to do. The ten companies of the First Colorado Volunteers donned their gear and began a fast, exhausting march on February 13, 1862, toward Fort Union. They traveled four hundred miles in thirteen days and arrived on March 10, where Colonel Slough assumed command.

While the First Colorado Volunteers were on their way, General Sibley had marched his Confederate troops up the Rio Grande and camped about seven miles south of Fort Craig. On February 16, Sibley sent a challenge to General Canby to engage in battle on the plains east of the fort. Canby initially declined but three days later sent Union troops out to meet their Confederate counterparts. The battle waged for the better part of the day until late afternoon, when the Confederates began to gain the advantage. Union soldiers retired to Fort Craig. General Sibley demanded the unconditional surrender of the fort, but Canby refused.

Sibley left Fort Craig behind and continued toward Santa Fe. The Confederate general was confident that he had cut Union lines of communication from Fort Craig but was unaware that 950 Colorado Volunteers had joined the 800 regulars and volunteers headquartered at Fort Union. Sibley collected supplies as he marched his troops to Albuquerque with no resistance. Confederate Major Charles Pyron continued toward

Santa Fe with 600 troops, similarly meeting with little resistance, as Union soldiers had taken what few men and supplies were there and moved everything to Fort Union. Pyron headed northeast with his troops and supplies and was camped at Johnson's ranch on March 25.

The road from Santa Fe northeast to Fort Union was one of the most heavily traveled as it was part of the Santa Fe Trail, then the major route across the country. A mountain pass is a geographic feature that provides an opening for access through more rugged terrain. Glorieta Pass was such a feature between Santa Fe and Fort Union. Ranches located at either end of the pass played significant roles in the upcoming battles.

Johnson's ranch was to the west of the pass, along Apache Canyon. Pigeon's ranch was just to the east of the summit of Glorieta Pass, and Kozlowski's ranch was farther to the east of the pass, not far from the Pecos River.

Colonel Slough had decided to confront their Confederate enemies at Santa Fe rather than wait for them and left Fort Union on March 22. Slough's forces then contained 1,342 men. Major Chivington was sent ahead with about 400 of them and reached Kozlowski's ranch around midnight on March 25, where he learned that Confederate scouts had been seen in the neighborhood. While most of the troops set up camp for the night, Chivington sent out a cavalry unit with 20 men to reconnoiter the area. They found and captured the Confederate scouts and brought them back for questioning, learning that the main force was just on the other side of the pass.

On March 26, Major Pyron left Johnson's ranch and encountered Union troops in the east end of Apache Canyon. After a fierce day of fighting, Chivington's troops had driven the Confederates back and captured a number of prisoners. One of the Confederates captured later wrote in a letter to his wife in Texas:

> *On the twenty-sixth we got word that the enemy were coming down the canon, in the shape of two hundred Mexicans and about two hundred regulars. Out we marched with two cannons, expecting an easy victory, but what a mistake. Instead of Mexicans and regulars, they were regular demons, that iron and lead had no effect upon, in the shape of Pike's Peakers from the Denver City Gold mines…before we could form a line in battle, their infantry were upon the hills, on both sides of us, shooting us down like sheep…They had no sooner got within shooting distance of us, than up came a company of cavalry at full charge, with swords and revolvers drawn, looking like so many flying devils…some of them turned*

> *their horses, jumped the ditch, and like demons came charging on us… Had it not been for the devils from Pike's Peak, this country would have been ours.*

As it became dark, Pyron sent word asking for a truce until 8:00 a.m. the following day while both sides buried their dead and collected their wounded. Chivington agreed, setting up a field hospital at Pigeon's ranch.

On March 27, reinforcement troops brought additional supply wagons and joined Major Pyron at Johnson's ranch. Pyron then had about 1,100 men at his command. Leaving the supply train at Johnson's ranch, the Confederates moved out on March 28 and stopped about a mile west of Pigeon's ranch to set up their battle formation.

Union Colonel Slough had joined Major Chivington at Kozlowski's ranch on the twenty-seventh and prepared for battle the next day. They devised a plan whereby Chivington would take four hundred men to the south across the mountains and flank the unsuspecting Confederates, harassing them from the rear, while Slough's remaining forces would confront them head-on near Pigeon's ranch.

On the twenty-eighth, Colonel Slough led his main units to the battle site near Pigeon's ranch, where Confederate guns opened fire. The main battle raged most of the day, with losses on both sides. Toward the end of the day, the Confederates began to gain a slight advantage. Colonel Slough ordered his Union troops back to Kozlowski's ranch, leaving the Southerners to hope for an eventual victory.

But during the heat of the battle among the rocks and trees, Chivington's men made their way across the mountains and got to the top of a bluff that overlooked Johnson's ranch, where Confederate supplies had been left under a minimal guard. The Union soldiers crawled or were lowered by ropes from the top to the base of the cliff. They then surprised the few Confederates guarding the wagonloads of arms and supplies and overtook them. All of the supplies were destroyed and burned, and even the mules who had pulled the wagons were slaughtered.

When the Confederate commander learned of the total loss of supplies, he requested a flag of truce from Colonel Slough. A few days were spent burying the dead and treating the wounded, but Confederate forces quickly retreated thereafter, their cause lost.

7
Agriculture, Floods and Locusts

The *Denver Rocky Mountain News* on May 10, 1862, printed the following:

From New Mexico
We have been permitted to peruse a letter, this morning, from Capt. R. Sopris, of the 1st Regiment, and below we publish a portion of the same:

Gallestillo, N.M., April 12, '62
We have saved this Territory, and perhaps Colorado, by coming here. Col Slough deserves a great deal of credit for our success. Had we remained at Fort Union until the enemy came up, I believe we would have lost many more men than we did; but as it is, we cut the enemy up so badly that they are leaving the Territory, and there are none of them north of Albuquerque.

We are about forming a junction with Canby, when we will drive the enemy from the Territory in a hurry.

I had the pleasure of seeing many of their officers and men, having met them under a flag of truce. The men, I believe, have been misled by their officers. The object of the campaign was for the purpose of plunder on the part of their leaders, many of them are gamblers, and have lived in Denver.

We have not seen Sibley, nor do I think we ever shall.

I saw 85 of their dead on the field. They had two hospitals that I was not permitted to go to. They have left at Santa Fe 85 of their wounded which were unable to be moved.

We lost the most of our men in the first deployment. The enemy were so concealed under cover of bushes and deep gulleys, that our men were deployed on them before they saw them. Companies D and I met their heaviest loss in that way. I lost my men in the afternoon. They attempted to flank us on our right, and Lieut. Chambers was sent with a platoon to check them. He suffered a severe loss, they charged in front at the same time. They retreated to Santa Fe and took what they wanted, got up an ox team and left. They are now at Albuquerque. We will give them a turn if they stay until we get there.

While the Colorado Volunteers were fighting the Confederates in a battle that became known as the "Gettysburg of the West," the federal government had removed William Gilpin as the governor of Colorado Territory and replaced him with John Evans. The new governor arrived in Denver in May 1862, just a year after Gilpin had taken office.

Governor Evans appointed a paymaster and charged him with honoring the drafts incurred by his predecessor for establishing the Colorado Volunteers. In spite of those efforts, many of them still remained unpaid. Evans later promoted Chivington, who had been instrumental in winning the Glorieta Pass fray. While both Governor Evans and Colonel Chivington are credited with influential decisions and actions in Colorado's early history, they were later castigated for parts they played in the November 1864 campaign against the Indians that became known as the "Sand Creek Massacre."

By September 1864, Elisha Milleson of the First Cavalry realized that Camp Weld was nearing the end of its useful service. He and his wife and children were living in a section of the barracks, so he filed a homestead claim on the land. The rest of the camp was disassembled for salvage. But the Milleson family converted the site into something of a park. They created orchards and fishponds and grew fruits and vegetables, which they sold at the local farmers' market. There was a swimming hole for summer activity that was converted to an ice skating rink in the winter.

Today, little remains of the camp. In 1934, a marker was erected to commemorate the site at 8th and Vallejo Streets in Denver with the inscription:

This is the southwest corner of Camp Weld. Established September 1861 for Colorado Civil War Volunteers. Named for Lewis L. Weld, First Secretary of Colorado Territory. Troops leaving here February 22nd, 1862 won victory over Confederate forces at La Glorieta, New Mexico. Saved the Southwest for the Union. Headquarters against the Indians 1864–65. Camp abandoned 1865.

Captain Sopris served in the Colorado Volunteers until July 1862, then returned to his family in Denver and took up farming on land in the Clear Creek area. Property records indicate that the Sopris farm was located near the confluence of Clear Creek and the South Platte River. That area is northwest of what is now Commerce City in the vicinity of 72nd and York Streets. Although there is a creekside trail in that vicinity and a pedestrian bridge that crosses Clear Creek close to its confluence with the South Platte, the surrounding area is mostly major highways and industrial development, including a sewage treatment plant. A house enclosed by a high fence along York Street may have been the Sopris farmhouse.

Sopris' first crops were beans, corn and potatoes. The Mexican pinto bean had been introduced in Colorado and became a staple in military rations. Sopris recalled that he had taken corn out of the feed boxes of his livestock and planted the kernels, getting a crop of roasting ears. Colorado-grown potatoes became a staple of many households.

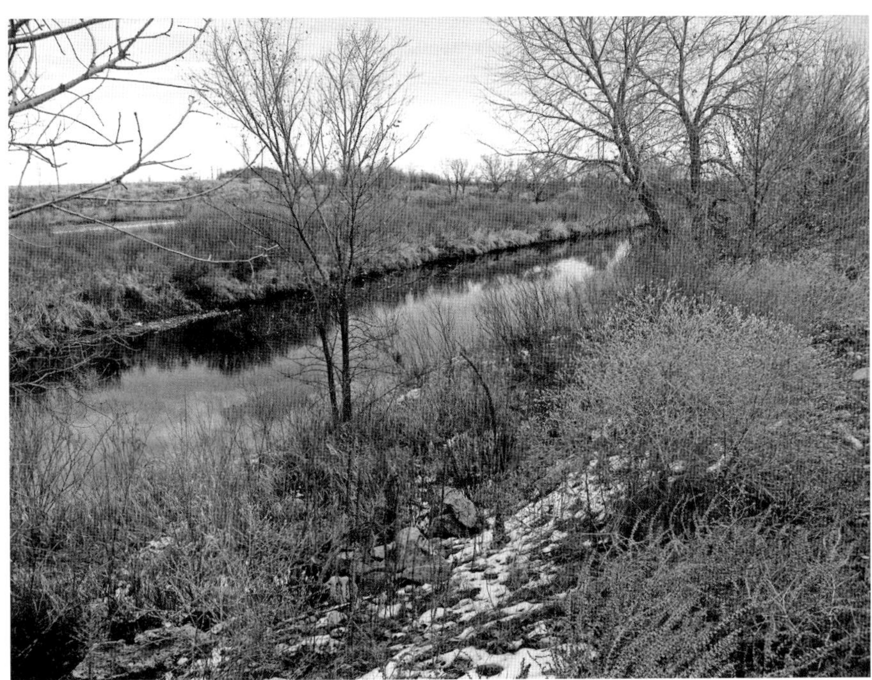

Clear Creek near the Sopris farm. *Photo by author.*

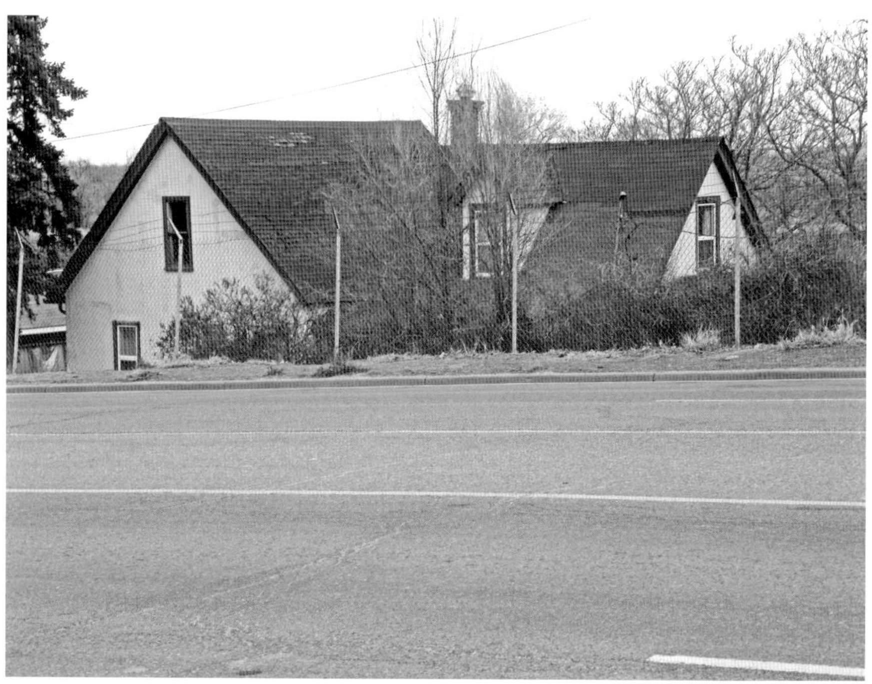

A house on the Sopris farm. *Photo by author.*

One of Sopris' neighbors, David K. Wall, lived near Golden in the Clear Creek area. Wall hadn't wasted any time trying to get rich mining gold but went right to his gardens. He diverted water from Clear Creek and laid out a hot bed for experimental gardening. He raised two acres of vegetables, which he readily sold in Denver. Sopris said of him, "He raised enough to prove to us that you could raise anything you could put into the ground if there was water to irrigate it."

Another neighbor of the Sopris farm near Clear Creek was Alexander Cameron Hunt. Sopris knew him from the Turkey War, in which Hunt had acted as judge for the Vigilance Committee. Hunt had brought his wife, Ellen, and two small children with him in 1859, and they subsisted by her efforts for a while. She took in boarders. She sold milk and butter from their cows, as well as bread and pies from her oven. Hunt planted oats and wheat and was successful with those for a few years.

Even though the early gold seekers had labeled the territory "the Great American Desert," some of them began to realize that the land was not as barren as they had first thought. Miners needed to be fed, and the price of shipping food was way beyond most of their means. Some of the early

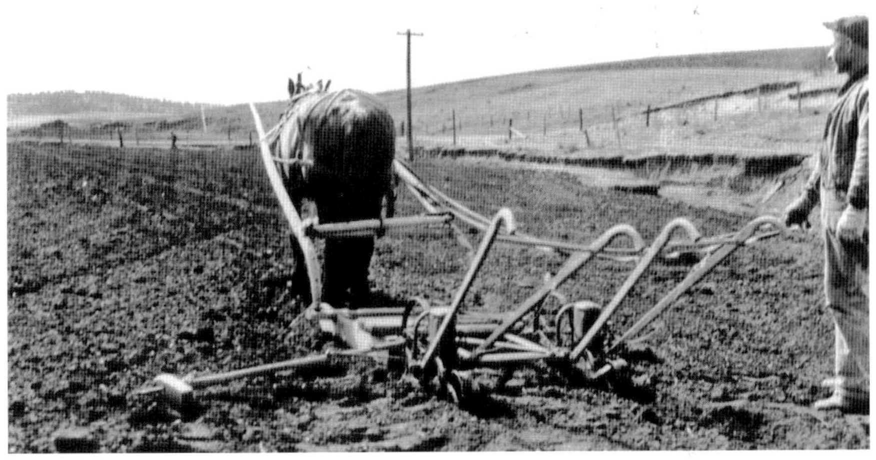

A horse and plow. *Courtesy of the Park County Local History Archives.*

arrivals began by buying worn-out oxen and feeding them back to health on the natural grasses. These were sold for meat to the hungry miners. Then a few, like Wall, began to show that commercial agriculture could be a paying proposition with proper irrigation.

As early as 1861, a notice in the newspaper encouraged a meeting of those interested in forming a Colorado Agricultural Society. Richard Sopris was among the early organizers, and a constitution was drawn up and passed in 1863. In 1866, Sopris, then president of the society, organized its first Agricultural Show. A forty-acre tract of land was purchased for the event. Stables were built to accommodate 110 horses, and pens were constructed to hold cattle, sheep and swine. An irrigation ditch ran through the property. A half-mile race track had been built, with a stand for judges close by. A few years later, Sopris entered some of his own draft horses at the fair.

William N. Byers was a huge proponent of the Agricultural Society and used his newspaper to promote it. During 1867 and 1868, Byers began to change his promotional theme to place agriculture and mining on equal footing. In his newspaper articles, he proclaimed that Colorado possessed not only a "mineral field, boundless as the human imagination in its rich resources," but also "an agricultural area that, in its superior yield of crops, has scarcely a parallel." He then reasoned that mining depended on farming and farming depended on mining.

The Colorado Agricultural Society became known as the Colorado Agricultural and Industrial Society. The fairs became an annual event. In 1867 and 1868, the annual fair expanded to include mining exhibits. In 1879, the Colorado Agricultural College began to admit students on campus at Fort Collins. Separate counties of the state individually organized their own fairs, and 4-H groups encouraged young people to become proficient at agriculture and ranching. County and state fairs still remain annual events in Colorado.

As farmers and ranchers well know, their occupation is not without its hazards and complications. A fire scourged much of the business district in Denver in 1863. Most of the businesses immediately began to rebuild. Then in 1864, another event more directly affected the farming communities.

From the earliest days of settlement, Cherry Creek had been a shallow-running stream, obediently staying within its banks. The people were so used to it that they had built their houses and businesses close to the waterway, some even in the middle of it. In May 1864, heavy spring rains began to mount up. From the mountain regions that flowed into the creek, the water flow turned into raging torrents.

The old city hall had been built in the creek bed. The flooding water took the building, along with the heavy safe bearing legal documents, and deposited it downstream, destroying most of the papers. The *Rocky Mountain News* and its heavy presses occupied a building with a foundation that consisted of stilts or posts in the creek bed. Several of the office employees were sleeping in the building and barely had time to rescue their personal belongings and escape before the swiftly running water carried their place of work into its depths. Two bridges were demolished, and houses were lifted off their foundations and deposited into the street. But the farming community also suffered. Stock and farm buildings were swept away. More tragically, human lives were taken; some were never accounted for.

One of the outcomes of the flood was a uniting of the two towns. Although they had both merged into the town called Denver, they had maintained separate identities. Many of the occupants living west of the creek, realizing that they were on lower ground, thus more susceptible to flooding, moved to the east side of the creek.

But nature was not finished with the farmers and ranchers of Colorado Territory. In 1865, a new and different scourge appeared. An innocuous insect that we often associate with the sound it makes when it rubs its legs together began to invade the land. Plagues of locusts or grasshoppers are not new. The eighth of the biblical plagues promised that locusts "will cover the face of the ground that it cannot be seen." And now the hungry insects invaded the fledgling territory of Colorado with a vengeance. Grasshoppers appeared in clouds and hordes, cleaning the ground of all vegetation. Crops and gardens were obliterated.

Grasshoppers invaded again in 1867 but not in such numbers. Then in 1875, the devouring insect again appeared in hordes. The streets and sidewalks of Denver were alive with them, and they invaded every building. Farmers and gardeners were stripped of everything, and many went bankrupt. Even railroad trains were affected; the crushed bodies of grasshoppers made the rails so slippery that the driving wheels simply spun around, stopping progress.

The offensive insect made its last devastating appearance in 1876 and has not caused a problem since. There are still grasshoppers around, but they are now noted as excellent fish bait.

8
Sheriff Sopris

On September 2, 1865, Arapahoe County held a convention for the purpose of electing county officials, including county superintendent of Common Schools, county sheriff, county attorney, county treasurer, county clerk and recorder, county surveyor, probate judge, county coroner, county commissioners and justice of the peace. Richard Sopris was by acclamation nominated for county sheriff.

There was even a jail now. For a while, a small log cabin on the west side of Cherry Creek had been used for that purpose. But in 1862, a building had been provided for use as a prison, located at 14th and Larimer Streets.

Since Denver's Vigilance Committee had gone out of business, the town was not quite as violent, but an element of vice remained. The gamblers had gotten so bold as to station themselves in the streets and entice luckless victims into their halls, where they were routinely fleeced for every cent they carried. The 1866 legislature enacted a law prohibiting every form of gambling, but the gamblers were simply driven underground.

Montana Territory still had an active Vigilance Committee. As Sheriff Sopris was assuming his duties, an incident in Montana Territory led the vigilantes to Denver.

The story was that a stage driver, Frank Williams, had colluded with road agents to ambush his stagecoach on the road between Helena and Salt Lake City in July 1865. Although all the passengers were massacred, including several prominent men, Williams remained amazingly unhurt. The robbers made away with about $60,000 in gold dust. In December, Williams took a leave of absence from his job as stagecoach driver and was seen in Salt Lake City spending gold dust. The vigilantes got word of this and went after him. Williams fled east to Denver and booked a room at the Planters House, a prominent hotel.

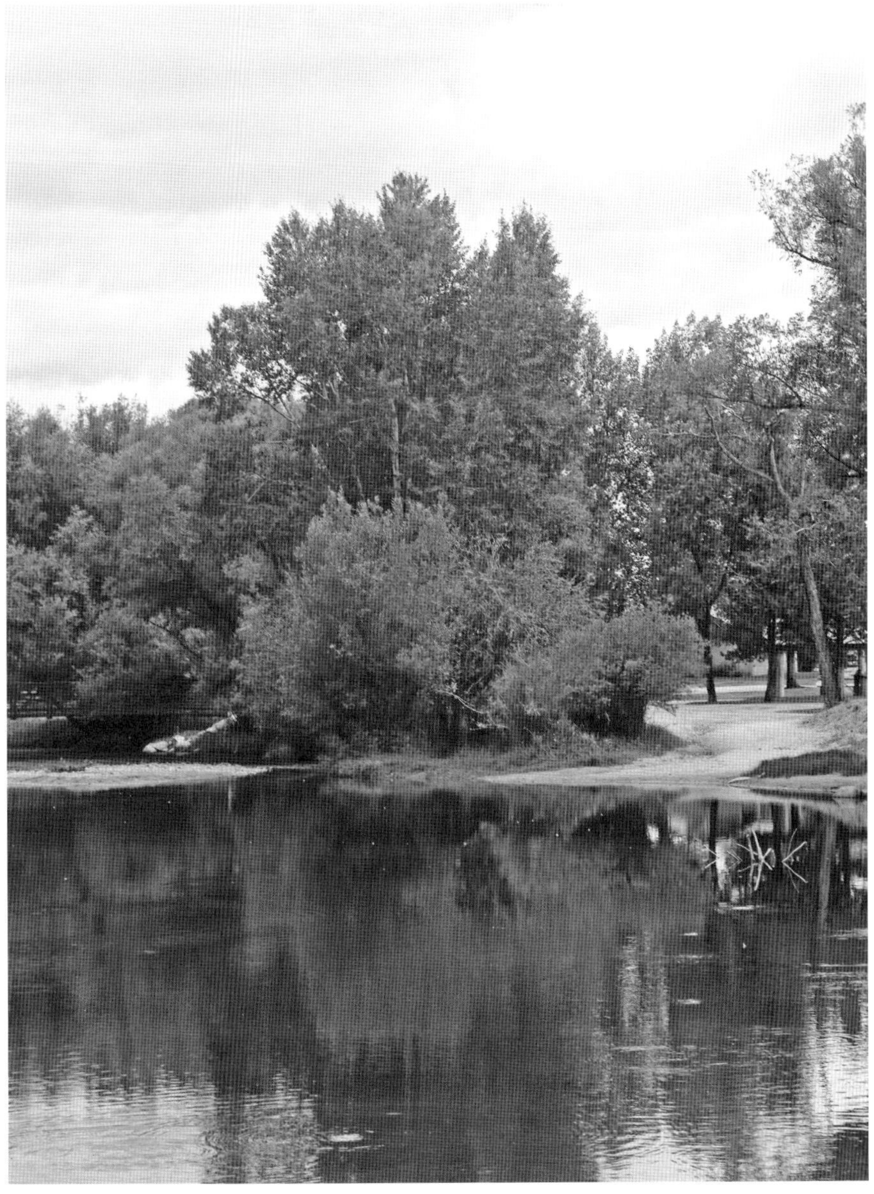

Cottonwoods along Creekside. *Photo by author.*

The vigilantes again followed him and approached the hotel. Williams recognized some of them and fled out the back door. He boarded a stage headed east, but the vigilantes were on his tail, chasing the stage with some fast horses. They caught up with the stage and stopped it, arresting Williams. He was brought back to Denver and incarcerated in the jail on 14th and Larimer.

A trial was conducted, during which Williams broke down and confessed his complicity in the massacre. The Montana Vigilantes took charge of him then. That night, they put him in a carriage and drove a short distance up Cherry Creek. They hanged him from a cottonwood tree. He was left with coffin-shaped papers and a red cross pinned to his body. Williams was buried under the tree from which he had been hanged, and years later, a plow turned up the bones.

On December 15, 1866, between 7:00 and 9:00 p.m., August Gallagher, known as "Cheap John," was brutally murdered in his own home. A simple, unoffending citizen, Cheap John was known to be a dealer in secondhand commodities. He was found lying on the floor upstairs in the building where his business was located. There were several wounds to his head that were thought to have been made with an axe or a hatchet. The victim lived for three days before he finally succumbed to the wounds without regaining consciousness.

In March 1867, George Corman was arrested and charged with the murder of Cheap John. A preliminary trial was held. Sheriff Sopris testified as one of the witnesses, asserting that he had suspected Corman of the crime but had found no direct evidence that implicated the man. The court decided that Corman should be tried for the crime of murder at the next term of the district court. He was held at the county jail to await the trial.

In May 1867, it was reported that ten prisoners had escaped from the jail. The escape was noticed by a lady in the neighborhood, who was so confused by what she saw that it took her fifteen or twenty minutes to decide that she ought to report it. This gave the escapees a head start, but it took only a day to recapture seven out of the ten runaways.

Granting an interview to journalists from the *Rocky Mountain News*, Sheriff Sopris took them through the jail. Sopris commented that it was a wonder how he managed to keep any prisoners there at all, the building was in such bad condition. The cell from which the ten prisoners escaped was one used during the day to confine those who were there for petty offences. The sheriff showed the journalists how easy it was for the men to pull up the floor planks with nothing but their hands, the floor was so old and rotten. The escapees went through the hole in the floor, then dug underneath a wall. From there they went into the stable, climbed out through a window and scattered in all directions.

The sheriff noted, however, that one prisoner remained behind. A fellow named Fitzgerald had been tried and convicted for murder and sentenced to be hanged, but his sentence was stayed after an appeal to the Supreme Court. Fitzgerald wisely decided that he was better off not attempting an escape.

Early in June, Sheriff Sopris and several law enforcement officials managed to apprehend a group of thieves who were making off with all sorts of livestock. Three of them were discharged for lack of evidence. Three more were charged with horse stealing and held for bail of $250 each. Another was charged with stealing six head of cattle; his bail was set at $300. They were all held in jail since they couldn't come up with bail money.

The sheriff noted that he was in possession of a team of mules that one of the thieves had stolen and would be happy to release them to their rightful owner.

Sopris still maintained his farm located on Clear Creek about four miles north of Denver. As sheriff, he was in contact with officials from neighboring counties, such as Weld and Boulder, and became aware of a problem with travelers from those areas who wished to come to Denver. Travelers had to cross the creek to get to their destination, and a few enterprising local fellows decided to take advantage of the situation. They built a poorly constructed bridge, known locally as Baker's Bridge, which forced most travelers to actually ford the creek, after which they were obliged to pay the huge sum of six dollars for the privilege.

The sheriff came up with a solution to the problem and in August 1867 accompanied the county commissioners to his farm, near which he showed them another bridge. He proposed to the commissioners that a road could be built from the bridge, which would not only cut off a number of miles for travelers from counties to the north but would be owned by the county and therefore provide a free crossing over Clear Creek. They all agreed that this solution would encourage trade between the counties. Construction of the road and improvements to what was commonly referred to as the Sopris Bridge began in September.

In January 1868, the trial of George Corman, accused of murdering Cheap John in December 1866, came before the district court. One of the chief witnesses was a young woman named Mary Kerwin. She and another woman had been living in the home of George Corman at the time, which was located a block from the residence and business of Cheap John. Mary testified that she was sick and lying in bed on the day of the murder. Corman had come into the house and asked where her tomahawk was. She replied that it was in the kitchen. Corman found the hatchet and left the house with it. When he returned several hours later, he asked the other woman, who was purportedly living with him as his wife, if she had heard the news. She replied no, and he said, "Cheap John is killed—he is not exactly killed, but he will never recover."

Corman went out and returned again with a little drawer filled with papers. He gave them to his wife and said to her, "They are of no account to me, they belong to Cheap John, and are bills he was going to collect; you had better burn them." The wife proceeded to burn the papers, and Corman broke up the little drawer, burning it as well.

Corman then took off his shirt and asked for a clean one. He threw the shirt he took off under the bed as he put on the other. He left again and didn't return for several hours. In his absence, the wife told Mary, "I am going to leave here soon, for George will surely be hung."

Mary recalled that on the morning after the murder, Corman was asked by the wife about the blood on the hatchet. Corman replied that it was chicken blood. Mary testified that she did not recall having seen any poultry in the house. She remembered retrieving the soiled shirt from under the bed and later attempting to bury it in a pot with some ashes. The shirt was retrieved and given to the coroner some six weeks later.

Deputy Sheriff Haskell testified that he and Sheriff Sopris went to Corman's house the day after the assault on Cheap John to ask questions. Haskell found the hatchet and noticed that although it was wet and appeared to be freshly washed, there was blood and hair on the end of the handle. Haskell then gave the hatchet to Sopris.

Sheriff Sopris testified that he had been notified about the assault on the evening of December 15 and went to Cheap John's quarters, arriving about the same time as the physician. Sopris looked carefully around the room, noticing that there were two work stands, one of which was missing a drawer. He noted the evidence of violence by the presence of blood on the wallpaper and a bundle of clothing on the floor.

Sopris and Haskell visited the Corman house the next morning. Sopris took the hatchet from Haskell, noticing what he thought might be human hairs on it. He and the physician compared the hatchet blade with the wounds on Cheap John's head and concluded that at least two of the three wounds could have been made with the hatchet.

The testimonies of three physicians and the coroner took up a great deal of time. The doctor who initially examined Cheap John explained in

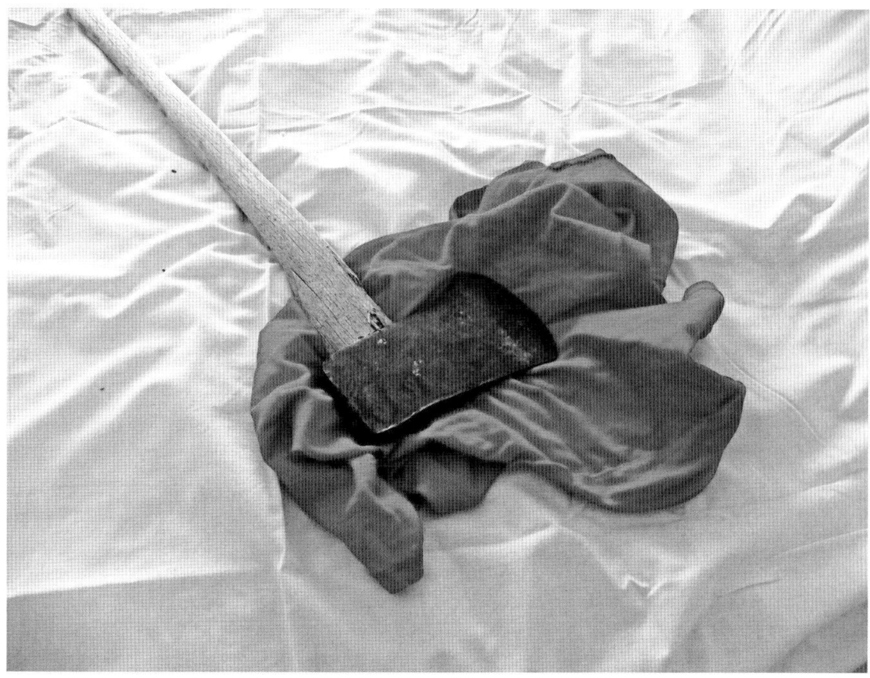

The murder weapon. *Photo by author.*

excruciating detail the size and character of the three wounds on the victim's head, indicating that the blade of the hatchet produced in the courtroom matched two of the wounds, and the third could have been made with the edge of the weapon. Questioning by the defense attorney revealed that the doctors argued whether the wounds could have been made by a pistol, hatchet, sling-shot or hammer.

The shirt that had been withheld from the initial investigation was examined for blood, which by that time had largely deteriorated. The discussion of the physicians then extended at length into the composition of blood and what effects time might have on the ability of the blood evidence to prove anything.

The attorneys finally made their closing arguments, and the case was submitted to the jury. The jurors had not made a decision by the end of the following day. There was no news of the verdict until May 23, when the *Rocky Mountain News* reported incidentally that the criminal docket had been disposed of: "Berkely, killing of Franklin, acquitted; Corman, killing of Cheap John, ditto..."

9

Railroad Contractor

After the end of hostilities from the Civil War, the country began to resume its growth and expansion into the West. The proposals for railroad routes that had been suspended now came up again. It had become apparent that a coast-to-coast transportation system was sorely needed and, with it, a system of rapid communication. It had been painfully obvious that a telegram with urgent news could get no closer than Julesburg and had to be relayed to the front by a courier on horseback. Shipments of goods from the coasts likewise took a great deal of time and money, as they had to be loaded onto wagons and driven across hundreds of miles of rough roads.

A transcontinental railroad was not a new idea. Congress had approved and conducted surveys as early as 1853 to determine possible routes from the Missouri River to the West Coast. And in spite of the chaos the country was in after shots were fired at Fort Sumter, Congress approved and President Lincoln signed the Pacific Railroad and Telegraph Act into law on July 1, 1862. The intent was stated in its title:

> *An Act to aid in the construction of a railroad and telegraph line from the Missouri river to the Pacific ocean, and to secure to the government the use of the same for postal, military, and other purposes.*

The act authorized the Union Pacific and Central Pacific Railroads to construct a continuous transcontinental railroad from the eastern side of the Missouri River opposite from Omaha, Nebraska, to the navigable waters of the Sacramento River in California. Land grants were awarded to the railroads in the form of "five alternate sections per mile" on each side of the tracks. Further, government bonds were authorized to be sold to finance the construction.

The land grants not only provided ownership of land for the railroads to build their tracks on, but individual parcels were to be sold to raise capital. Farmers and settlers were eager to buy the land so they could locate close to the railway stations.

The question now was which route across the country to the west would be best for the railroad. Union Pacific engineers had surveyed possible paths and settled on a route that followed the Platte River west, veered north through Cheyenne, across the Rocky Mountains and through Bridger Pass in southern Wyoming Territory. This route was longer in miles, but the terrain was not as rugged as one that crossed the Rockies near Denver. Besides, federal subsidies were given by the mile, so more miles meant more money in the railroad coffers.

What this meant to Denver and Golden was that any railroad line through either town would be a branch, not part of the main line. Thus there would be no government financing, and the individual counties would have to fund the building of the railroad lines to connect to the main lines to either coast.

Those two towns had been competing for the attention of railroad routes, and both tried to get the route for tracks laid to maximize their own interests. Golden had managed to get the appointment as capital of Colorado Territory in 1862. The legislature would typically meet in Golden and then adjourn to Denver, where there were better facilities. Finally, the Colorado Territorial Legislature declared Denver to be the capital in 1867.

Denver promoters were dismayed at the Union Pacific selection of the northern route but immediately began looking at other options. Golden promoters responded by proposing a link from Cheyenne to Golden by way of the Colorado Central Railroad, which they had chartered in 1865 and reorganized in 1866. Union Pacific officials looked at several routes that covered the mining areas and the towns of Golden, Denver and Boulder. Any of the proposed routes would have required financing from all of the counties affected. Bond issues put to the ballot could not pass in all of them, so the Colorado Central Railroad plan was defeated.

Meanwhile, John Evans, who had served as governor until 1865, continued to promote a railroad directly between Denver and Cheyenne. Evans was born near Waynesville, Ohio, in 1814 to parents who were descendants of an old Quaker family. Evans grew up on the family farm, then went to Clermont

Academy in Philadelphia, where he obtained a degree in medicine in 1838. He practiced medicine for a number of years. His interests expanded to railroad construction, and he was active in developing the Chicago & Fort Wayne Railroad. He also took an interest in politics and helped Abraham Lincoln get elected president, which led to his appointment as the governor of Colorado Territory to replace William Gilpin. Evans was implicated in the infamous Sand Creek Massacre, which occurred in 1864, and he in turn was replaced as governor by Alexander Cummings in 1865.

Evans' interest in seeing the railroad developed in the territory, however, did not abate. He was a member of a committee established to cooperate and confer with Arapahoe County commissioners regarding the development of a railroad line to Denver. He and a number of Union Pacific officials had developed a plan to provide Denver a railroad connection by means of a line extending from Cheyenne to Denver and from there into the mining districts. To that end, a bond issue was proposed.

In the midst of these negotiations, the Kansas Pacific Railroad suddenly appeared on the scene. The Kansas Pacific was a nominal subdivision of the Union Pacific and had obtained government subsidies to extend its lines from Kansas City westward. Several routes to the southwest had been explored, and Denver promoters had assumed that the Kansas Pacific would extend in that direction, thus avoiding a line directly into their town. However, the government subsidies for the Kansas Pacific had run out, leaving the line stranded at a terminal in western Kansas.

As the Kansas Pacific examined its options, a plan to connect with the Union Pacific from Denver emerged as the most viable one. John Evans conferred with Kansas Pacific officials about the connection and saw the possibilities. He engineered the creation of a new "Board of Trade" in Denver in 1867. The Board of Trade proceeded to look at financing possibilities, and the Denver Pacific Railroad and Telegraph Company was created. Capital stock was issued, and many local promoters invested in it.

A contract for constructing the Denver Pacific was agreed upon with the Union Pacific in Cheyenne, whereby the Denver Pacific would grade the surface and prepare the roadbed and the Union Pacific would provide and install the rails, then furnish the rolling stock. Construction would begin at both ends. A ceremonial breaking of ground was held on May 18, 1868, at a point not far from the current Blake Street and Fortieth Avenue in Denver. Initial grading that extended from Denver to the Platte River crossing was completed before the end of 1868.

The Union Pacific, however, had not even started from its end at Cheyenne. Upon a demand from Evans for an explanation, the Union Pacific people pleaded financial inability. The Denver Pacific had contracted with a local company to build a telegraph line between Cheyenne and Denver, and that was completed on January 1, 1869.

At Evans' urging, a bill was introduced in Congress to authorize the Kansas Pacific to build to Denver and terminate there. The Kansas Pacific was also authorized to cooperate in the completion of the Denver Pacific line to Cheyenne. Land grants and bond issue capabilities were extended to both lines. The bill passed on March 5, 1869. All of this now put the railroad lines on a substantial financial footing, and work then proceeded from the northern end of the line, extending south to the Platte River crossing to join the track that had been built from Denver.

A town was developed at the meeting point and appropriately named Evans. November 1869 found Richard Sopris in that town. The *Rocky Mountain News* reported, "The railroad bridge is to be planked for the use of teams until the railway goes on. Captain Sopris has the contract, and the work will be done as soon as the plank arrives."

It was also noted that Captain Sopris owned a number of the properties in the town of Evans that had been offered for sale by the railway company. The town had been laid out with 1,200 lots, and between sixty and seventy buildings had been erected or construction was underway. Structures included a hotel, three or four boarding houses, three corrals, ten or twelve stores, two barber shops and a number of saloons.

One of the hotels was the scene of a shooting early in November. A man named Joel Carr was upset because he had to wait for his dinner to be served and began to verbally abuse Daniel Steele, the proprietor. Steele tried to dissuade Carr, but the disgruntled customer became even angrier and left, only to return with his revolver. The implacable customer then fired, hitting Steele in the head and killing him. Carr threw away the weapon and ran out, heading toward Denver. He didn't get far before he was caught and brought back to town. A people's court was immediately empanelled, and Captain Sopris was called upon to act as judge. The jury quickly found the shooter guilty of first-degree murder, and the judge sentenced Carr to be hanged from the nearest tree. The sentence was carried out, and it is presumed that the hungry murderer never did get his dinner.

Captain Sopris continued to work on the grading in preparation for the railroad tracks to be laid. He was also responsible for the grading where a siding would be built to the nearby colony town of Greeley. The concept of colony towns was to build a cooperative venture, selling equal shares to inhabitants, with all the labor, capital and profits to be shared equally by the members. The town of Greeley was one of the few successful ones, but not without its share of problems. It did not help matters in Greeley when the town of Evans began its colony only a few miles away. Greeley's founders made a hard and fast rule that intoxicating liquors were strictly forbidden. The colony town of Evans openly allowed grog houses and taverns within its limits. Both towns survived after their colony charters expired, but Greeley won the contest for becoming the county seat in Weld County.

The Denver Pacific Railroad was completed, and the first train arrived from Cheyenne to Denver in June. The ceremony of driving the final spike was conducted with a silver spike donated by the miners from Georgetown. The spike was engraved on one side: "Georgetown to the Denver Pacific Railway"; the other side was engraved: "John Evans, President, June 24, 1870." The celebration included a full day of processions, music and speeches.

The Kansas Pacific was not far behind. Although construction crews were periodically plagued with Indian attacks, the tracks were finished, and

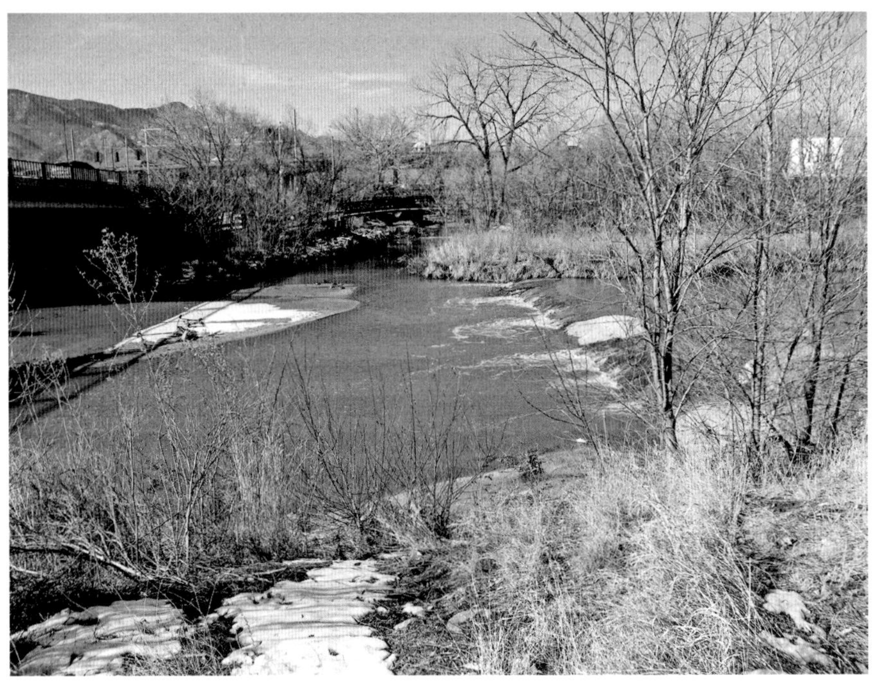

The confluence of Fountain Creek and Monument Creek. *Photo by author.*

the first train arrived on August 15, 1870. This completed a connection for Denver traveling and shipping to the East and West Coasts.

William J. Palmer had been on the staff of the Kansas Pacific until its completion to Denver. He then resigned so he could begin work on his own plans to launch another railroad extending south from Denver. Palmer's dream was to connect to El Paso, Texas, and eventually to Mexico City. The Denver and Rio Grande began construction in March 1871 and by October had reached a spot near the junction of Monument Creek and the Fontaine qui Boille, or Fountain Creek. From there, Colorado Springs was laid out. Palmer envisioned that the town would one day become a fashionable summer resort.

When the railroad was finished to that point, one house marked the spot: a low, flat, mud-roofed log cabin hotel kept by Captain Richard Sopris. The rude frame building was "elongated like a rope-walk, and about as imposing in appearance as a bowling alley." It was referred to as "The Log Cabin" and was the first hotel in Colorado Springs.

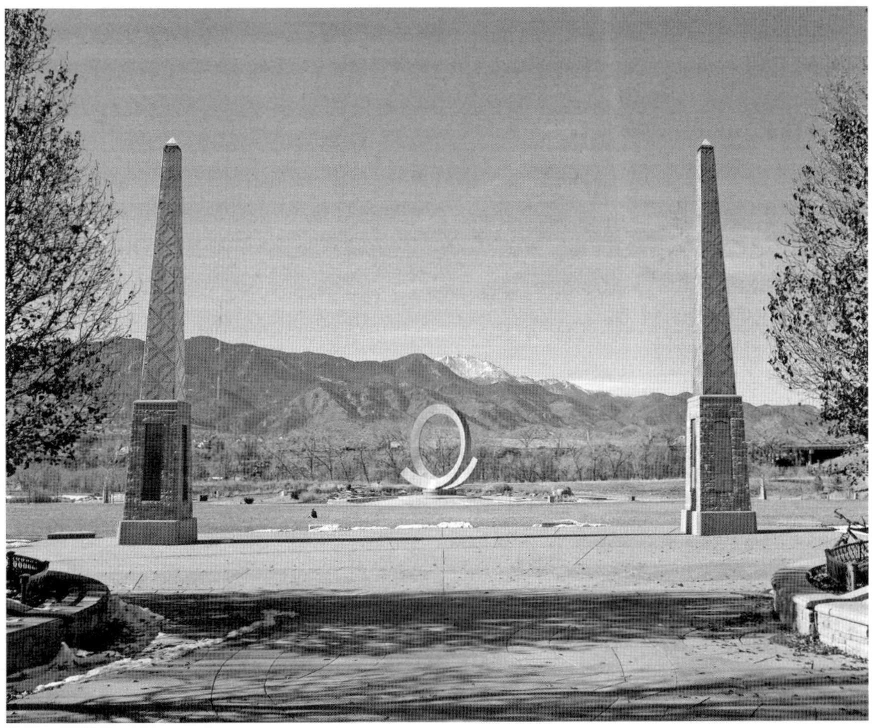

America the Beautiful Park. *Photo by author.*

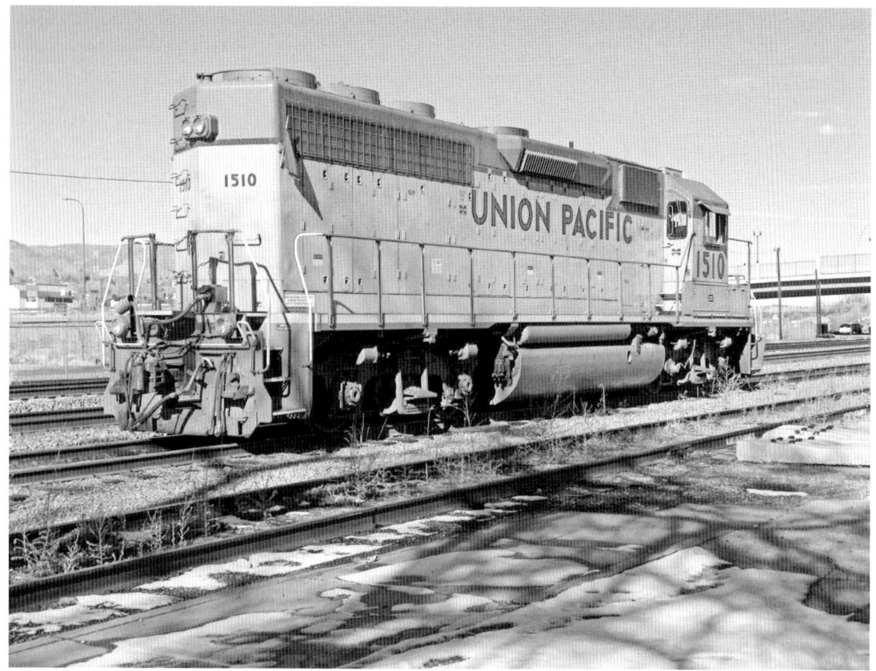

A Union Pacific train on tracks near the Colorado Springs depot. *Photo by author.*

The hotel has long since disappeared, but a park has recently been developed at the edge of the confluence of the two creeks. It used to be called Confluence Park but has been renamed America the Beautiful Park. Built to be a "greenway" along the creeks, the park includes a multiuse trail that connects with a countrywide trails system. Nearby there are still a few trains that use the same railroad tracks as those that were first built to connect Colorado Springs with the rest of the country.

10

Warden Sopris; Colorado Is a State

Captain Sopris was still in the Colorado Springs area in December 1871 and hadn't left behind his law enforcement skills. On December 8, two prisoners managed to escape from the county jail in Denver. A bulletin was telegraphed to all the neighboring towns, so all citizens were on the lookout for Mike Hennesey and Charles Hiller, the two crooks on the run.

Both of them headed for Colorado Springs, and Hiller was apprehended by former Sheriff Sopris, who then placed him in the charge of Denver officers. Hiller was shackled in irons and placed on board the narrow-gauge train headed to Denver. Soon he made an excuse that he had to visit the water closet. Once inside, he closed the door and raised the tiny window, then managed to jump out. His unique exit was noticed by some passersby, who immediately reported the incident. The train was stopped and backed up to the spot where Hiller still lay. He had injured himself in the fall from the train to the point that he could not get up and run away.

He was picked up and returned to the train, which again proceeded toward Denver. Hennesey was caught in Colorado Springs a day or two later and similarly transported north for continuing incarceration, although he didn't attempt the water closet window escape. Both resumed their stay in the quarters at the Larimer Street "black hole," the name by which the jail was commonly known.

Captain Sopris was appointed jailer (or warden) of the Arapahoe County Jail from 1872 to 1875. During that time, his son Levi, known as "Lee," worked as a guard in the jail. One incident that involved both

Soprises began late in 1872. The *Denver Daily Times* reported on January 18, 1873:

> *...on the 21st of December a young man from Idaho named John Aikens lost a team at the Cricket in the usual manner of that establishment. The father, Dennis Aikens, came down here, and aided by members of the police force, instituted a search for the team and investigation. The team was found some miles out of town, and restored to the owner. A charge of grand larceny was made out against John Chase, Tom Mason, Gordon Brown and Albert Schroeder.*

The Cricket was a place of amusement, famous for its shows and infamous for its gambling tactics, which relieved many a patron of his possessions. The theft of the mules came to be known as the Cricket Mule Robbery. The roustabout at the Cricket testified as to the guilt of the four, and they were all indicted for grand larceny. Brown broke out of jail and got away while awaiting trial. Schroeder was acquitted, it appearing that he was the mere dupe of the others, and Chase jumped the bail bond.

The last of the four, Thomas Mason, went to trial in October 1873 and was convicted of larceny. His attorneys attempted to get a new trial but failed. So on December 1, Mason was sentenced to three years in the penitentiary. He was still in the Arapahoe County Jail on December 8 when he and a fellow inmate managed to escape.

The deputy on duty that evening thought he heard whispering noises in an adjacent cell, but an examination revealed nothing unusual. However, some time between three and five o'clock in the morning, the escape was made from the cell directly above the one examined. Mason and his cohort picked the lock to their cell, then the one next to it, in which there was an air hole to the roof. It was not known where they got the instruments to pick the locks, but there was evidence that they wrapped the links in cloth to muffle the noise. From the roof, the two jumped to the ground and were off.

Sheriff Willoughby received word that Mason was spotted in Medicine Bow, Wyoming, and telegraphed the authorities to pick him up. The evasive thief was heavily laden with irons and transported back to Denver on the Denver Pacific Railroad. By December 20, Mason was again a guest of that loved institution on Larimer Street.

On January 3, 1874, the county jail awoke once more to find that Mason and another inmate had escaped. This time, it was suspected that there was outside help, as there were holes cut in the ceiling of the ground-floor cell, the cell directly above and the roof above that.

The escape was again conducted so quietly that Lee Sopris, the guard who happened to be on duty that night, heard nothing unusual but the wind. The *Denver Daily Times* reported that "the need of a new jail will now more forcibly than ever come home to the inhabitants of the county." Mason was apprehended once more and successfully transported to the penitentiary in Canon City on January 12.

A bond issue had been put to the voters to provide money for building a new jail, but it took two efforts to finally get approval for the county to spend $50,000 on it. Approximately $8,500 was spent to purchase the land bounded by Colfax, Santa Fe and West 14th Avenues and South 11th Street. A contractor was hired, and the new building was started immediately.

The *Denver Daily News* reported on August 6: "Seven days have elapsed since the last arrival took place at the county hotel on Larimer Street. Captain Sopris, the proprietor, says that nearly all his boarders are those that are bound over and he don't want any more until he gets into the new quarters."

The new county jail was completed and ready for use on September 5, 1874. The new premises did not quell the intent of those incarcerated to escape. Early in December, Sheriff Willoughby and Jailer Sopris pried open the lining of a prisoner's boot and found the stub of a knife that had been nicked or notched like a saw. Using his hidden weapon, the inmate had made some headway sawing through one of the iron bars.

In spite of their attempts to recover possible escape devices, the sheriff and jailer were caught unawares as four jailbirds managed to saw through iron bars and slip through them and out the back way. They had picked a time—noon—when only the guard was there. Sopris and other authorities puzzled over how the criminals obtained tools to so efficiently break them out of the new jail.

That mystery was not solved. Six months later, in July 1875, another bold escape made the headlines. Again, Sopris and the sheriff were both out. The jail was manned by two guards, Lee Sopris and Edward Holtz, who were in the office or reception room with the door to the cells open so they could hear what was going on. Suddenly, a gang of seven inmates rushed through the door and attacked the guards. Holtz was beaten severely and rendered bloody and unconscious. Lee Sopris, "being a powerful cuss," had attempted to grab his revolver but was overcome by the marauding criminals. It took four of them to beat him to the floor. The seven escapees had rounded up the cook as well, dragged both guards and the cook into an interior cell and locked them in before they left the jail.

The two ringleaders of the brutal attack were awaiting trial for murder. They were well known as leaders in a gang of thieves and desperadoes. Somehow, a saw had been spirited into the jail, and they used it to saw off one of the iron bars in the corridor. A piece of the bar was used as a bludgeon on Holtz, whose injuries nearly resulted in his death. Lee Sopris was taken to his home in an express wagon to recover from the bruises on his arms and back.

While the Sopris family was experiencing these traumatic incidents, the U.S. Congress had passed an Enabling Act, which gave general guidelines for the legislators of Colorado Territory to create and submit to voters a constitution. This was the pathway for Colorado to graduate from a territory with no representation and no votes in the U.S. Congress to a state. Previous efforts had been unsuccessful, the reasons given that there was not enough population to support designation as a state.

Stipulations in the Enabling Act required the state constitution to adopt the Constitution of the United States, that it be republican in form, that it make no distinction in civil or political rights on account of race or color (except Indians were not to be taxed) and that no language would be repugnant to the U.S. Constitution or the Declaration of Independence. Further, two specific stipulations were made: one, that there be tolerance of religious sentiment and two, that all unappropriated lands within the territory would belong to the federal government.

The thirty-nine delegates to the constitutional convention began to wrestle with the document they would eventually produce. One of the first controversies that came up was whether or not God should be recognized. The delegates finally came up with the first sentence in the Preamble: "We the people of Colorado, with profound reverence for the Supreme Ruler of the Universe..."

Other questions that were thoroughly debated involved taxation of church properties and regulation of railroads. And then there was the question of women's suffrage. Many of the delegates wanted Colorado to be the first state to legalize women's votes, in addition to being the state organized on the centennial of the nation's birth. But more were conservative and afraid that voters would not approve that drastic a movement. They did make a concession that women could vote in school elections.

The constitution was submitted to a vote of the people on July 1, 1876. Although the vote was fairly light, it being the busiest season for farmers and miners, a count found the ballots overwhelmingly in favor. The constitution was immediately submitted to the U.S. Congress. Although the official act of the U.S. president's signature of approval didn't happen until August 1, the people opted to used July 4 as the day of their celebration as the Centennial State.

Ceremonies planned for that day involved just about every civic organization in Denver. The parade included military, firemen and Knights Templar. One of the most conspicuous groups was the Argonauts of '59. The group had organized under the name of Pioneers' Association, and its members included such personages as William Byers, Judge H.P. Bennet, Professor Goldrick and, yes, Captain Richard Sopris.

It was a proud day for Colorado, as exercises were held at the Denver Grove, near Cherry Creek, where some of the first settlers began their lives in the mountains amongst the gold seekers.

II

Mayor Sopris

In 1877, the Colorado State Legislature grappled with one of its first problems: when to hold elections. They attempted to schedule state elections to coincide with city elections. The City of Denver had traditionally held election of city officers in April each year. In 1876, the mayor of Denver was elected in April, but his term ended in October of the same year. The next mayoral election resulted in a one-year term ending in October 1877.

Changing of election dates and terms of office resulted in confusion and differences of opinion among those in judiciary positions. Finally, it was made public in the local newspaper that Captain Sopris had asked Judge Rockwell to research the matter and publish his opinion. After a wordy and circuitous discussion, the judge concluded that the newly elected officials could legally take office in spite of other opinions to the contrary.

At the 1878 October election of city officials, the *Denver Daily Tribune* reported, "The election of Mr. Sopris, the Republican candidate for Mayor, was a foregone conclusion, and he was elected for the position by a most flattering majority."

The year 1879 was one of growth and innovation in the city of Denver. Railways, telegraphs, water and gasworks, street cars, fire alarms, telephones—all were now available in the capital city. One of the few conveniences citizens did not have was free mail delivery. It was approved in Congress but so far hadn't happened. In April of that year, William N. Byers was appointed postmaster of Denver. He was one of the first newspaper owners and editors in the area but had sold the *News* the previous year.

Byers took over the post office when there were long lines of customers waiting in front of delivery windows for hours to retrieve their mail. He began by establishing letter boxes throughout the city and appointing six letter carriers. Denver began to be competitive with other major cities in postal efficiency.

The year 1879 also marked the occasion when two of the largest hotel complexes were built. The Tabor Block was purchased by H.A.W. Tabor, and no expense was spared in building a structure that was five stories high, the upper stories reached by elevator. It was designed to be the finest building west of Chicago. The other hotel built that year was the Windsor Hotel, which boasted diamond dust mirrors, marble floors, miles of Brussels hand-carved furniture and everything necessary to make it the most famous hostelry in the West.

But every city has its problems, and for Mayor Sopris the two largest were Cherry Creek flooding and the sewage system (or lack thereof).

As early as 1875, the city had attempted to take some control of Cherry Creek by suggesting that Denver purchase the old ditch leading to Capitol Hill. The resolution failed at first, but a special election in May 1875 was successful, and the city purchased the property. The ditch supplied water for use in underground conduits across the Capitol Hill plateau. Various plans were submitted to reroute the creek and discourage the destructive flooding that had happened in the past. Plans were even approved, but bond issues failed. In May 1878, the rains again caused the creek to rise and carry with it most of the bridges along its path. The bridges were cheaply built of wood and became part of the debris. They were later replaced with properly built iron structures.

The sewage problem came to a head in 1879, when an outbreak of typhoid fever caused the city to face the situation. A leading physician reported his first typhoid patient that year. He described the living conditions of the patient, who had recently come to Denver and was in the process of building a house on the banks of Cherry Creek. The physician surmised that the bed of the creek probably served as the family privy.

Conditions in 1879 were ripe for an epidemic. The summer was dry, and water levels in the Platte River were low. Primitive sanitary facilities were inadequate for the increase in population. Denver had no sewers. Housewives threw their refuse into nearby ditches. Merchants discarded their outdated meat products the same way. If it weren't for the roaming dogs, chickens, hogs and other animals, all the refuse would have rotted in the ditches. But while these animals took care of some of the trash, they left

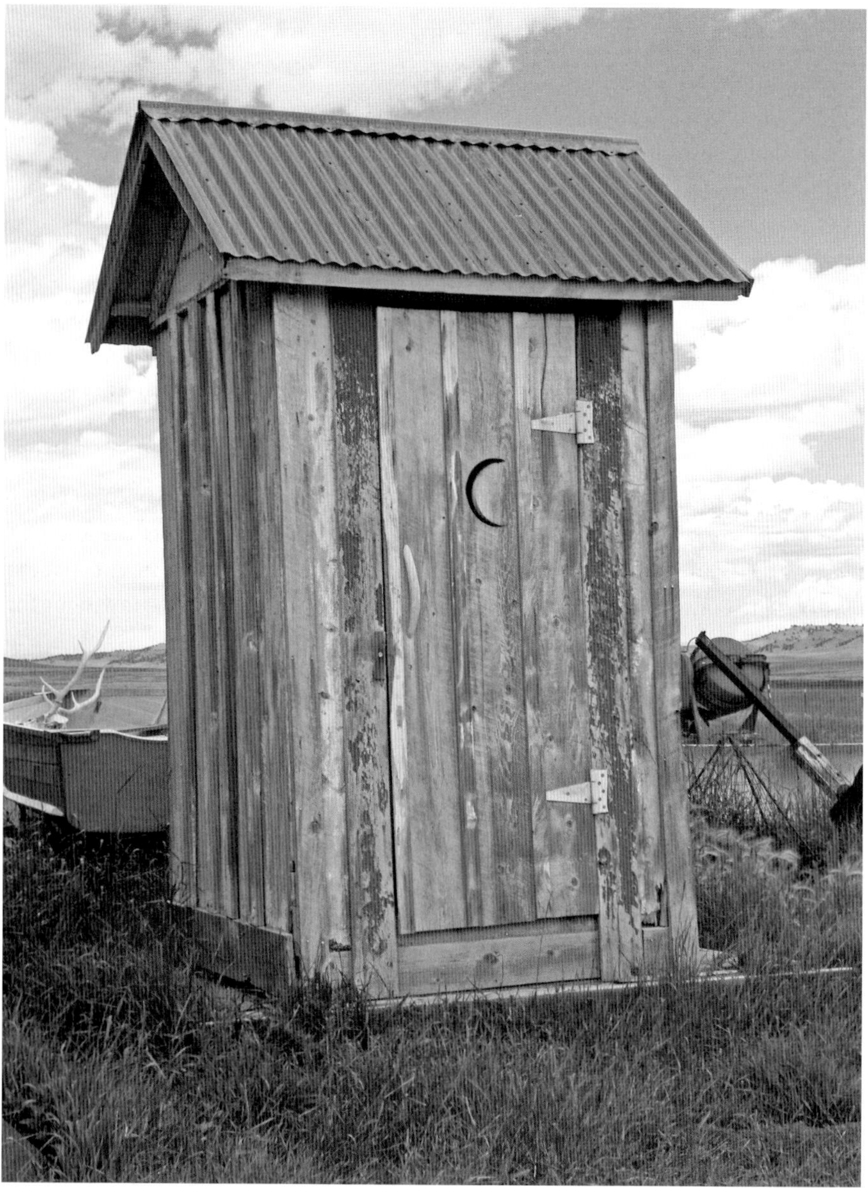

An outhouse or privy. *Photo by author.*

their own rotting refuse behind. The only time the ditches were cleaned out was during a rainstorm.

Human waste went into privies behind the homes that were seldom cleaned. Eventually, the waste flowed underground into nearby water supplies. Refuse from the jail and at least one hotel was piped directly into the ditches and the creek. Although the city government had routinely passed measures to establish a system of sewerage, nothing appeared to get done.

Mayor Sopris was reelected in October 1879, and his remarks at the installation ceremony addressed the necessity for action on the sewer system by the new city council:

> *The vote on sewers at our last election affords simple endorsement for immediate and effective action on constructing the same. I would suggest that you do not permit the grass to grow or snows to fall before excavated trenches shall show the earnestness of your purpose to fulfill the wishes of your constituents.*

As cold weather approached, the epidemic subsided. The plan for an adequate sewage system developed by the city engineer was adopted in December. Sewer tax districts were laid out, work began and the system was put into operation in 1880. This was not to be the end of challenges for Mayor Sopris.

Chinese laborers had been imported to work on the railroad lines as they were being extended into the western reaches of the country. Some of the Chinese then migrated to the mines to work. A community of Chinese had made its way into Denver, and they subsisted mostly by doing laundry and other menial tasks. They stayed for the most part in their own community, which became known as Hop Alley.

They were regarded with much suspicion, as their customs were vastly different from the rest of the population. They dressed differently, and they all sported the traditional que—a braid of hair down their back—which showed their allegiance to the country they had left. They were hated by the laboring class, as they worked more cheaply than the average working man and cost many of the white people jobs that they thought they deserved. The situation in Denver exploded on the night of Halloween in 1880.

A couple of railroad workers had just collected their wages and come to town to spend their money and have a good time. They found their way to a saloon with billiard tables that was frequented by the Chinese. Two of the local Chinese were playing a game of billiards when the ruffians began harassing them. One of the railroad workers hit a Chinese fellow over the head with a billiard cue. One of the Chinese then fired a pistol, the shot hitting no one. The railroad workers lost no time in inciting the local public to attack any and all Chinese.

When Mayor Sopris got word of the riot going on, he drove to the scene and tried to disperse the crowd. He was without a chief of police at the time, as that personage had been suspended in a disciplinary action. The mayor then called on the fire department to hose down the crowd, thinking that would cool them down. It only served to anger most of them, and they continued to ransack houses and commercial buildings, looking for Chinese to harm.

The police force at that time consisted of only twenty-five or thirty men, not adequate to quell such a mob. Luckily, David J. Cook was in the area and realized what needed to be done. Cook was then chief of the Rocky Mountain Detective Association. He had previously been sheriff of the county, a soldier, a scout, a detective and, most importantly, had access to a number of troops he could call on.

Mayor Sopris quickly assembled the City Council and appointed Cook the acting chief of police. He notified the local military to be on standby. Cook took his men and began to infiltrate the angry crowds. He instructed them not to kill, but to shoot into the ground, then immediately raise their smoking pistols to eye level. In this manner, the angry mob began to disperse. Most of the Chinese residents were hurried to the county jail and locked inside for their protection. A few were caught out and chased by the ruffians with murderous intent.

Not all of the white community, however, was on the warpath with the Chinese. A notorious gambler and desperado, Jim Moon, faced the crowd and protected one of the Chinese who had not managed to find safety. Moon pointed his pistol at the crowd and let them know that "this Chinaman does my washing, and 'By the Eternal' you shall not harm a hair of his head." The leaders of the mob knew Moon's reputation and opted to turn around and spare their prey that one time.

The madam of a local brothel protected four Chinese with her shotgun pointed at the crowd. She was backed up by about "ten Amazonian beauties" from her establishment, all armed with champagne bottles, stove pokers and high-heeled shoes. When the fire department showed up, too, the unruly members of the crowd lost their courage and began to leave. By the end of the rioting, there were at least thirty-four Chinese sheltered in the brothel.

One old man, Sing Lee, had gotten caught out in the fray in the vicinity of 19th and Lawrence Streets. He sank to his knees in the face of the crowd and was rewarded with vicious kicks and blows. A rope was then put around his neck, and he was dragged down 19th Street. After the mob left him, he was taken to a nearby doctor's office, but medical efforts could not save him.

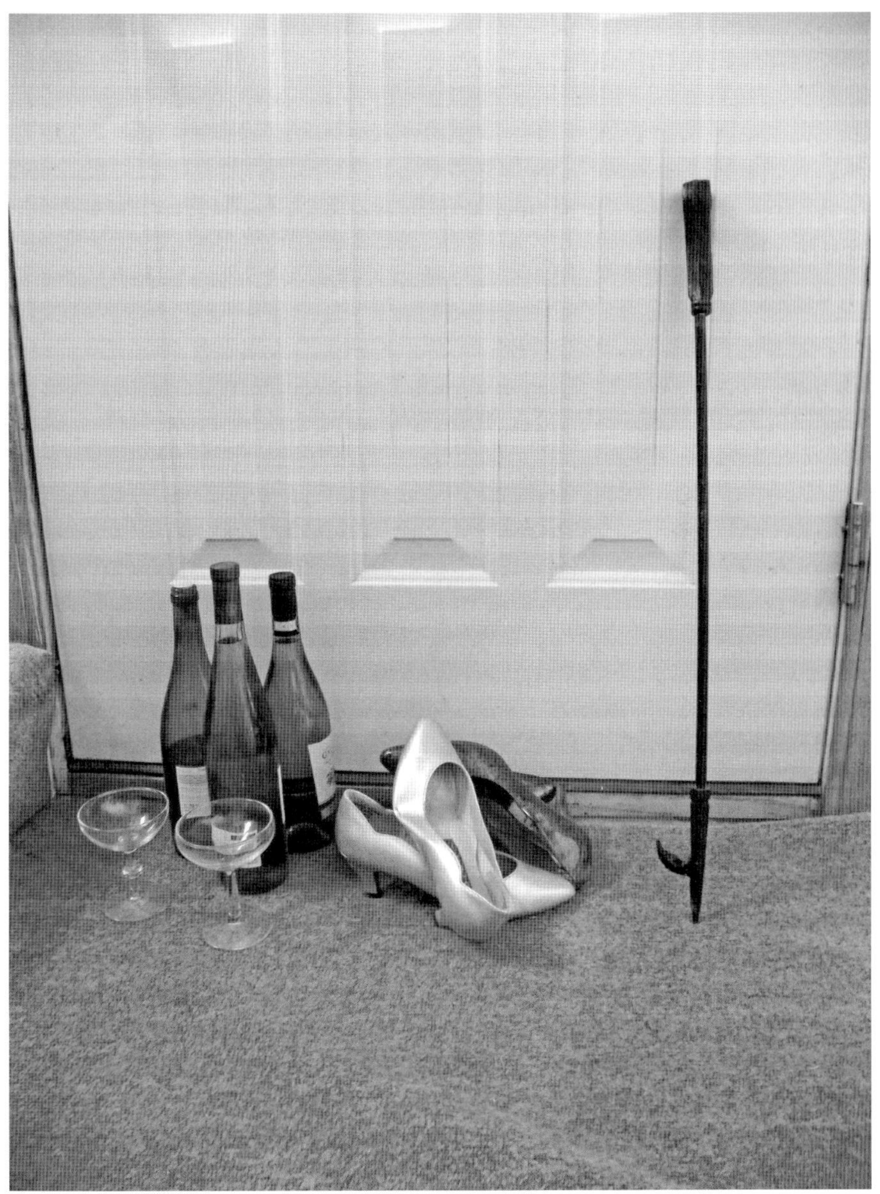

Weapons to defend the Chinese. *Photo by author.*

A number of the rioters were ultimately arrested. But very few of them were convicted, most of them released because of insufficient evidence. More than $30,000 in claims were filed, but actual Chinese property losses were estimated at $53,655.69.

There is a historical marker in Lower Downtown Denver on Wazee Street about the Hop Alley/Chinese Riot of 1880. It is part of a walking tour depicting Denver history.

12
Denver's City Park

Jerome Smiley wrote in 1901 in his *History of Denver*:

> *The pioneer founders and platters of the city had practically made no provision for parks…It is quite probable that if anyone had suggested to them the actual need for city parks on their plats, they would have concluded that a far greater and an immediate one existed for a small asylum for insane advisers.*

Before leaving the office of mayor, Richard Sopris suggested in a letter to the *Rocky Mountain News* that the citizens of Denver consider approval of a plan to buy land to develop as public parks. He indicated locations for half sections of land in four different areas, divided up in such a way as to be close to most residents of the city. He advocated renting some of the land for agricultural purposes, additionally requiring the tenant to plant trees. The total area in his suggested plan was 1,260 acres, or 320 acres per parcel for each park. The City Council reduced the acquisition of land for a park to a single 320-acre parcel. City Council members ratified the park land purchase on February 18, 1882.

After Sopris concluded his term as mayor in 1881, he was almost immediately appointed Denver's first park commissioner. One of his first challenges was to figure out what trees would grow. In the area designated for a city park, the soil was quite alkaline and subject to disease and pests not conducive to healthy trees. Sopris called upon a newcomer to the area, Henry Meryweather, a civil engineer, to help with initial plans for a city park.

The land was surveyed, and a plan presented to the city included pathways for horses and foot traffic through the park. There would be formal gardens, statues, fountains and other amenities similar to those that had been introduced in New York City's Central Park. A portion of the ground was set apart for a "nursery maids' walk." There was no mention, however, of how the nursery maids would get to the park over the rough ground from the homes of their charges.

Sopris settled on cottonwood trees for an initial planting. He solicited $500 in contributions from owners of adjacent properties to purchase the trees. He purchased more out of his own funds. To maintain the young saplings, he hired a German gardener to live there and chase out any nibbling animals. The gardener worked for $10 a month and his rent.

A tradition from the neighboring state of Nebraska was borrowed: the celebration of Arbor Day. On that day, schoolchildren were encouraged to make a field trip to City Park and plant trees.

Sections of the park were inundated with weeds. Sopris came up with the idea to lease those acres to a sharecropper. The land was planted with oats, which thrived in the soil. The city actually made money from its share of the crop.

Denver put to use land that had been purchased in 1875 to augment the City Ditch. Channels from the ditch brought water to one of the areas in the park that later became Duck Lake. An island was developed in the middle of Duck Lake that became a breeding ground for several species of waterfowl.

Many of the trees were planted in an area that was not reached by channels from the City Ditch. An artesian well was installed to bring water to hundreds more of the trees.

The Denver Tramway Company established service to City Park and sponsored bands for musical performances at an area where a pavilion would be built. For a while, there was a floating bandstand where musicians bobbed along in the big lake, entertaining park visitors.

In the early 1880s, it became fashionable for young gentlemen to challenge one another to horse and harness races. They began racing up and down 17th Avenue, which soon became a menace to pedestrians and regular traffic. The racers were ordered off the public thoroughfares. But upon application to the city, they were granted use of a section of land on the northeast corner of City Park. Using their own funds, they built a grandstand and a race track for their amusement. In 1898, the grandstand collapsed. The grandstand was not replaced, but a new sport was introduced as the Gentlemen's Driving and Riding Club was organized. Then there were auto races at the park. By World War II, the race track had outlived its usefulness, and the land was reclaimed for purposes more suitable to City Park.

Among the many attractions developed in later years was the zoo, whose beginning can be traced to a bear cub given to Mayor Thomas McMurray in 1896. The bear cub was given to the park teamster, who chained the animal to a haystack for the entertainment of park guests. The teamster also was trying to raise chickens, not many of which survived the whims and appetites of the bear. So a cage was built and decorated with a bear house and a bear pool.

Another feature of City Park came much later, around the turn of the century, when the collection of natural history displays of Edwin Carter were obtained by the city, and the Denver Museum of Natural History was opened.

In 1886, the Richard Sopris family celebrated the fiftieth wedding anniversary of Richard and Elizabeth, who were married back in Indiana in 1836. Some five hundred invitations were sent out to people, most of whom attended the Golden Wedding Anniversary party at the Sopris home. Although the invitation specified that no presents were to be brought, a few elegant floral offerings made their way onto the parlor mantel. An orchestra provided music for the entertainment of the guests, but there was scarcely a square inch to be had for any dancing. A list of the attendees looked like a who's who of local officials and important people.

Captain Richard Sopris performed the duties of park commissioner for about ten years but reluctantly gave up the position in 1891. In 1893, the Office of Park Commissioner was replaced by a Park Commission consisting of three officers.

In April 1893, Captain Richard Sopris, at the age of eighty years, became ill and passed away at his Denver home. He left his widow and six of his eight children, two of whom had predeceased him .

One of the Sopris sons, Simpson T., decided to memorialize his father by building a gateway to City Park, on which the captain had worked for ten of his last years. The structure is a pedestrian and trolley entrance off 17th Avenue. The Richard E. Sopris Gateway was to establish a lasting testimony of the public-spiritedness of a man whose accomplishments should not be forgotten. The inscription listed his accomplishments—pioneer, miner, legislator, explorer, soldier, sheriff, mayor and park commissioner. Today, the gateway still stands, but the inscription plates are no longer there.

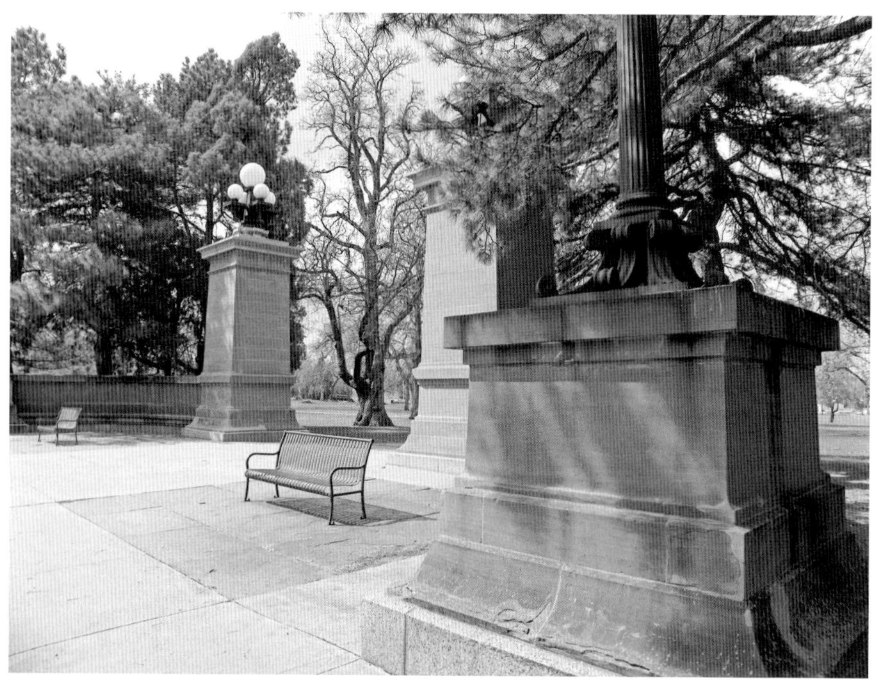

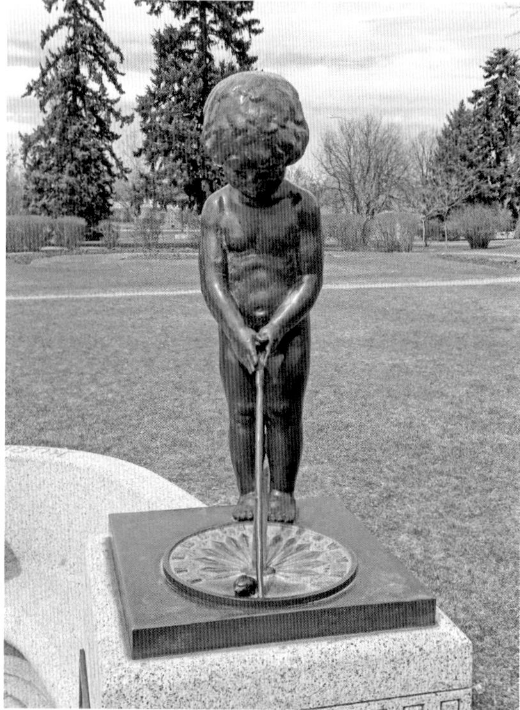

Above: Sopris Gate at City Park. *Photo by author.*

Left: The sundial at City Park. *Photo by author.*

Simpson then erected another memorial in 1925 to remember his mother, Elizabeth, after her passing in 1923. The statue depicts a small boy at whose feet lies a sundial. The inscription is to Elizabeth Allen Sopris. It is located behind the pavilion at City Park.

13

The Rest of the Family

Elizabeth Lloyd Allen was born on February 15, 1815, in Trenton, New Jersey. The daughter of Thomas and Irene Allen, she is said to be a direct descendant of Revolutionary War patriot Ethan Allen. He was famous for being one of the founders of the state of Vermont and colonel commandant of the Green Mountain Boys, a militia company that helped capture Fort Ticonderoga in the early years of the Revolutionary War.

Elizabeth remembered that when she was only nine years old she and a score of other little girls dressed in gala attire and assisted in welcoming the French hero Marquis de La Fayette. The girls strewed flowers in his path as he made his way through Trenton, New Jersey, on a historic tour of the United States. La Fayette, a close friend of George Washington, had influenced France to assist the new nation in winning

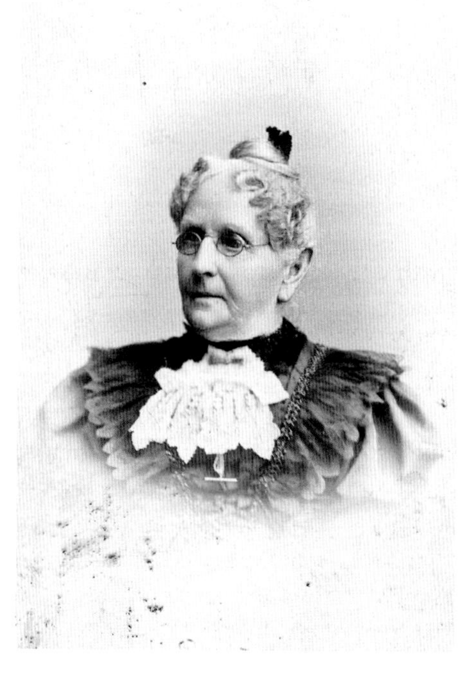

Elizabeth Sopris. *Courtesy of the Farrington family.*

its war against the British. He then came to America to help fight the war. In 1824, President James Monroe and the sitting Congress invited La Fayette to tour all twenty-four of the states that made up the nation at that time in honor of the fiftieth anniversary of the birth of the United States.

Shortly after her twenty-first birthday, Elizabeth met and married Richard Sopris. They went to live in Indiana, where they were blessed with eight children. When Captain Sopris (the title first given to him when he captained riverboats on the canals) became interested in going west to explore the Colorado gold fields, Elizabeth stayed behind in Indiana with the children. In 1860, he had made up his mind that his future was in the West and went back to Indiana to collect his family.

They traveled by train, riverboat and wagon, arriving in Denver in April 1860. They first lived in a log building on Ferry Street. Mrs. Sopris recalled their first Christmas there. "There was no tree with its glittering ornaments, no buying of expensive presents—but a gift of some little thing each one desired," she told the *Denver Post* when the newspaper wrote about her fiftieth Christmas holiday in Denver.

She also related a "laughable incident" that Christmas involving her two daughters. At that time, fruit was an expensive commodity, and bon bons were worth their weight in gold. A suitor, trying to impress one of the Sopris girls, brought a gift in a cardboard box containing apples and bon bons. He paled when she began distributing them amongst the other callers at the Sopris home. Taking the girl aside, he reminded her that the apples cost twenty-five cents each and were meant only for her.

On their first New Year's Day in Denver, Mrs. Sopris recalled that they held an open house. Her particular memory was that it was such a balmy day that the doors and windows were opened to permit the sun to stream in. It was January 1, 1861.

Not long thereafter, the Civil War broke out. Captain Sopris was again given the title "Captain" as his rank with the Colorado Volunteers when he took over Company C. Mary Sanford was the wife of Lieutenant Byron Sanford, the quartermaster of Company H. She was one of the few wives who attempted to follow their husbands during their assignments with the military. The volunteers were garrisoned at Camp Weld as they were organized. In her diary, Mrs. Sanford noted that "the spot occupied by this camp is on the same ground where the Russell brothers discovered gold in dry Creek about July 1, 1858."

Two of the companies, Company C and Company H, were notified on December 1, 1861, that they were to be sent to Fort Wise (now Fort Lyon), a military post about two hundred miles from Denver on the Arkansas River. Arrangements were made for Mary to travel with the two companies. They settled in for what they thought might be a long stay. But on March 1, 1862, messengers brought orders for the two companies to depart and join the rest of the companies of the Colorado Volunteers on their way to Fort Union to encounter Confederate troops heading that direction from Texas.

Mary didn't know what she was going to do, but Captain Sopris solved the problem. "You are to go to my home. I will write to my wife." Mary's diary then related, "Here I am, taken in by dear Mrs. Sopris until something else turns up."

She further explained, "She [Mrs. Sopris] keeps the Officers' Mess and I am to assist her some in the dining room, or not do anything unless I choose, but I feel so much better to be employed…"

A son was born to the Sanfords while they were living at Camp Weld. He would grow up to become the assistant curator of the State Historical Society. Albert B. Sanford contributed greatly to the historical memories of Camp Weld and was instrumental in seeing that the monument was erected at 8th and Vallejo Streets in Denver in 1934.

While her husband was involved in political activities and other pursuits, Elizabeth Sopris pursued her own activities. She was one of the twelve charter members of the Congregational Church of Denver, organized in 1864. Daughters Indiana and Irene were also among the first charter members. A church was built at 15th and Curtis Streets in 1870.

In 1875, the Sopris family moved into what would be their home for more than thirty years. The address was 1337 Stout Street.

In 1886, Mr. and Mrs. Richard Sopris celebrated their fiftieth wedding anniversary by hosting an event that entertained many of those who had come to Denver in its early years and stayed to help the city and state prosper. There were, no doubt, many reminiscences shared that evening.

Captain Sopris, whose last accomplishment was to establish City Park in Denver, became ill and passed away on April 7, 1893.

Elizabeth Sopris spent much of her time working with the Ladies Aid Society. She became known as the "Grand Old Lady" of that organization. She expressed her hope to live to be a hundred.

But three years shy of that goal, she developed bronchitis and succumbed to it on December 18, 1911.

Allen B. Sopris, the oldest of the Sopris children, was born in 1837. He wanted to join the Union Army but was unable to because of a physical disability. He was twenty-two years old when the Sopris family left Indiana to make their new home in Denver in 1860. Shortly after they arrived in Denver, Allen accompanied his father and the group of people who explored the area near where Glenwood Springs is now. When the group split up and Captain Sopris opted to head east toward home, Allen went with the recorder, D.C. Collier, and Dr. Arnold, now a group of sixteen, who elected to continue south.

The prospectors had to cross the Grand River in a different location than where the *Western Wanderer* had been built, and they couldn't use the boat that had been cached. So they built another boat. The river was very rapid there, so they searched several miles for a place to cross. Finally, they decided to try the boat. Unfortunately, they had to go over a rapid, which caused the boat to upset. They lost axes, hatchets, a whipsaw and guns into the waters, and two of them made for the shore. Another stayed with the boat, clinging to it as it went downriver another two miles, where he was able to push it to shore. They salvaged what they could and repaired the battered boat. They were finally able to cross the river with their animals but without many of their tools.

They continued traveling south and finally came upon the road that they recognized as a wagon road from Salt Lake to Fort Garland. Now traveling southeast, they began to run short on provisions and were on the lookout for some sign of civilization. One morning, they chanced on a lone ox feeding at the river. They briefly checked the ox for signs of ownership but butchered the animal anyway. After they had eaten their fill of beef, they discovered a brand on its hide indicating that the ox was probably the property of "Uncle Samuel."

Several days later, they came upon the sight of the "Stars and Stripes" fluttering in the breeze over Fort Garland. Allen was able to post a letter to his father dated October 24.

From there, Collier headed north back to Denver. Dr. Arnold's group planned to go northwest toward the San Juan Mines, and Allen went with another group to Albuquerque, from where they hoped to get to the San Juan Mine as well.

The San Juan Mines were promoted by a man named Charles Baker, who was later described as a "restless, adventurous, impecunious man who was always in search of something new." Baker prevailed upon a couple of financiers to outfit him and six others to explore the country along the Animas River. They set out in July 1860, traveled south over Cinnamon Pass and along the Animas River to where Baker claimed to have discovered rich deposits. The area was named Baker's Park, later to become the town of Silverton.

Baker then traveled south to Abiquiú, a trading post in New Mexico, where he loudly proclaimed the richness of his find. This started what became known as the Baker Expedition. Many hopeful prospectors began to infiltrate the San Juan area. A camp, called Camp Pleasant, was set up near Cascade Creek, a tributary of the Animas River. And in a more hospitable area downriver, a town was laid out and named Animas City.

Dr. Arnold and his party of twenty-four left Fort Garland in November of 1860, headed for the San Juan Mines. They somehow missed Baker's trail and instead took an old Indian trail that led them into the Uncompahgre Valley. There they were forced to winter. They were, however, well provisioned and survived by killing some of their draft animals for meat. Then, short on draft animals, they had to modify their wagons into carts. They took off again in the spring and eventually stumbled into Animas City. Unfortunately, they arrived about the time that most of the inhabitants were packing up to leave, having been disappointed in their gold findings.

Allen Sopris left Fort Garland about the same time as the Arnold party, headed for the San Juan Mines via Albuquerque. He was held up at Abiquiú due to the illness of one of the members of their party. Allen wrote to his father that "reports were very encouraging, and if they were properly supplied with pack animals, they felt confident of getting through without trouble." While he was in Abiquiú, he observed that it was "a miserable Mexican village, with supplies, and the very worst starting point at which to start over the mountains."

The party finally reached Animas City at the end of December 1860. The party agreed at that point that "if those are all the discoveries that Baker has made, they are worthless, and Baker is either deceived himself, or the most outrageous deceiver that ever lived." Allen soon thereafter made his way back home to Denver.

In 1867, it was announced that Allen Sopris had married Ellen Jernigan, daughter of a leading newspaper owner and editor in Michigan City, Indiana. The couple traveled overland in a stagecoach to their home in Denver.

Allen served a single term as the city assessor in 1868. In the early 1870s, he opened and ran a bookstore, selling stationery, wallpaper, pens and other items in addition to books, magazines and newspapers. A frequent ad was printed in the local newspaper:

DENVER BOOK STORE
POSTOFFICE BLOCK
ALLEN B. SOPRIS

In August of 1874, the same newspaper reported that the bookstore had been burglarized, the thief taking between $600 and $700 worth of items. The burglar apparently tried to get in through the transom on the back door and, failing that, carved a hole in the door, then reached inside and turned the key. There was also a prop that had been pushed up against the door, which the thief shoved aside to gain entrance. The most valuable items taken were 450 gold pens, worth about $3 apiece. Also missing were items from the jewelry store that occupied the front end of the shop.

In October 1874, Allen submitted a piece to the newspaper entitled "Clean and Fix Up." He encouraged customers to fix up their homes with brand-new wallpaper, then adorn the same walls with "exquisite chromos and paintings," all available at his place of business. He then suggested that customers "obtain the latest magazines, novels and newspapers, as well as the standard works of living and dead authors" for their libraries.

It was reported in 1883 that "Messrs. C.J. Stewart and Allen B. Sopris had purchased the entire display of the Abbott Buggy company, and also the agency in this state for that company." After the exposition, the new owners would occupy the old Archer hose building on Curtis Street.

Allen was finally forced to discontinue his business because of a severe kidney disorder, which caused him a great deal of pain. He kept active in current affairs, however, and continued to periodically meet with friends and acquaintances. In March of 1897, he wrote to the *Rocky Mountain News* about a recent coverage of the Espinosa incident that had happened back in 1863. The fellow who had apprehended the Espinosas, a tracker named Tom Tobin, had never been paid the reward that was due him. Allen contacted the governor of Idaho, Governor Shoup, who had been the commanding officer at Fort Garland, near where the outlaw had been caught and killed. Shoup remembered that there had never been a payment and forwarded $200 to Allen, who then got in touch with people who knew where Tobin was currently living. The money was forwarded to Tobin, a much-delayed reward.

It was a scant two months later when Allen B. Sopris was relieved of his pain, as he passed away in May of 1897. He left his wife, Ellen, and all four of their children—Belle, Charlotte, Frances and Allen Jr.—to grieve their loss. The funeral was conducted by the Colorado Pioneer Society, of which Allen had been a longtime member.

INDIANA SOPRIS, the oldest daughter of the Sopris family, was not quite twenty-one years old when the family began their trek west. Born on July 12, 1839, Indiana had already gained some experience as a teacher in the

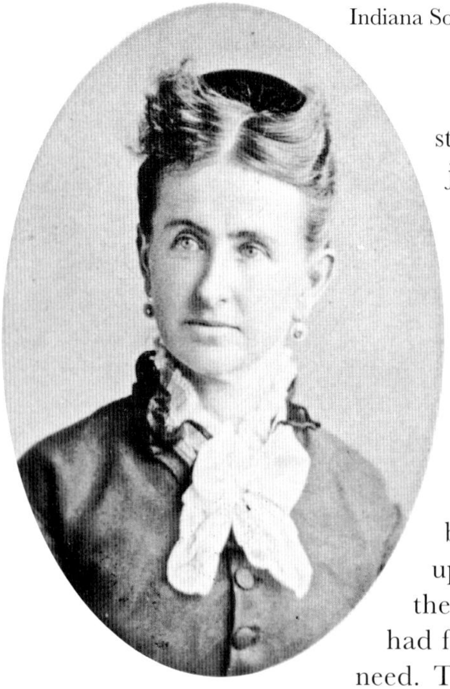

Indiana Sopris. *Courtesy of the Farrington family.*

state that bears her name. She kept a journal of their trip from their home at Michigan City, Indiana, until they reached the town of Denver, Kansas Territory.

They traveled by train and riverboat until they reached Atchison, Kansas. There they picked up their belongings, which Captain Sopris had shipped to that point. The day before they were to leave, they set up the ten- by ten-foot tent and slept the night, a trial outing to see if they had forgotten anything that they might need. The girls, their mother and father bedded down in the wagon, and the boys slept in the tent, along with a companion, Mr. Young.

Indiana related occasions where they met young men who were traveling the same route and passed the Sopris wagon. She appeared somewhat flirtatious, as well as eager to see what adventure might come next. She also wrote of Indians they met along the way. All of them were curious and friendly. She told of one chief who shook hands with everybody in the camp and proudly showed her a piece of carved cedar that someone had printed his name on. She noted in her diary that the name "Dig-Belly" did not seem too stylish a name.

Her diary entries complained of the wind and rainy weather. A week before they came to the end of the journey, Indiana wrote, complaining of the wind blowing sand and dirt into their eyes: "Our very worst day out and I do hope we may not see another such. Put us all out of tune and temper. Father and I had a spat."

She then wrote, "Think I'll try to behave in the future."

As they neared the end of their journey, she wrote of the large number of emigrants they began to meet. The last entry was made on April 23, 1860.

The Sopris family took up residence in a two-story log house in Auraria, now West Denver, on Ferry Street. Only two weeks after their arrival, Indiana again became involved in teaching. In addition to her own younger brothers, she found a number of families with children needing the "discipline and training of a school." As she looked for a suitable building for the school, she approached Thomas Pollock, a local blacksmith, who owned a building at the end of the same block on Ferry Street where the Sopris family lived. She began teaching her class on May 7, 1860, which at first consisted of only ten or fifteen students. The class soon expanded to as many as she could handle.

Indiana declined to claim the honor of being the first teacher in Denver, as O.J. Goldrick had already set up a school known as the Loggery. Goldrick was a rather colorful character who wore a broadcloth suit, a stovepipe hat and kid gloves. He had been educated in Ireland and at Columbia College in New York. He supplemented his income as a correspondent for eastern newspapers.

But Indiana Sopris was the first woman schoolteacher in Denver. She was still teaching in 1863 when she began keeping a diary again. The entries in this diary are much shorter than those in the original one. The name "Cush" keeps cropping up in her frequent entries. It was apparent that she was keeping company with one Samuel Cushman, a civil engineer who made frequent trips to the east and into the mountains with his business. The Cushman family traced their roots back to the original Plymouth colony in America.

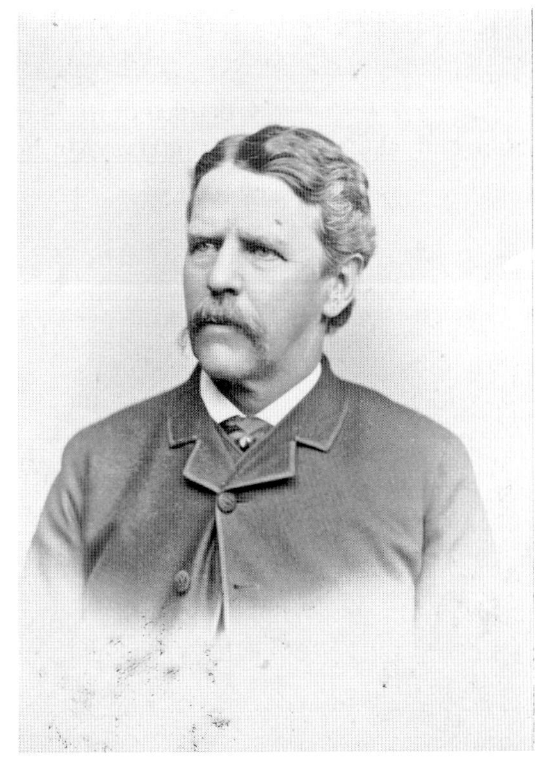
Samuel Cushman. *Courtesy of the Farrington family.*

The couple married in 1866 and set up house in Central City. A neighbor there remarked of "a beautiful bride stepping out of a carriage near the rose-brown granite steps of a very new frame house on East First High Street." In 1867, Irene, the first child of the Cushman couple, was born; then a son, George, three years later.

The family moved to Caribou, a small mining

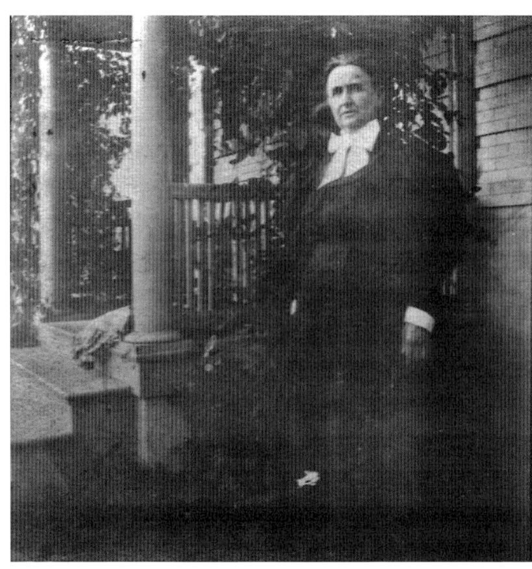

Indiana Sopris Cushman. *Courtesy of the Farrington family.*

town near Nederland, where Samuel became the superintendent of a silver mine. A daughter was born to them there: Charlotte. In 1878, Samuel became an agent for the Hazzard Powder Company, and they moved to Deadwood, then a part of the Dakota Territory.

Samuel Cushman passed away in 1899, and Indiana returned to Denver to live with her mother and two of her brothers who still resided at the Stout Street home. She lived there until her passing in 1925. She had been named an honorary president of the Pioneers of Colorado.

Irene Sopris was born in 1841, the second daughter of Captain and Mrs. Sopris. When the family arrived in Denver in 1860, Irene began to teach Sunday School. She and her mother and older sister were original charter members of the Congregational Church.

John Sydney Brown had come west with his brother Junius, and the two started a freighting outfit in 1859 that traveled from Kansas to Denver. In 1861, J. Sydney opened a grocery business in Denver. It was wiped out by the 1863 fire and again by the 1864 Cherry Creek flood. That same year, a twenty-wagon train bearing goods intended for the Brown store was destroyed by Cheyenne Indians just as it was reaching the outskirts of Denver. J. Sydney obtained a line of credit and ordered another stock of goods for his store. He and his brother Junius partnered to organize the J.S. Brown Brothers Mercantile Company.

In 1868, Irene Sopris married J. Sydney Brown. The two had five children together: Fred S., Edward V., William K., Elizabeth B. and Katherine B.

Early in January 1881, Irene was seriously ill. By the end of the month, she had expired at the young age of thirty-nine. Her brother George, who was at that time a court justice, adjourned his court for several days. Her father, who was then mayor of Denver, did not attend the City Council

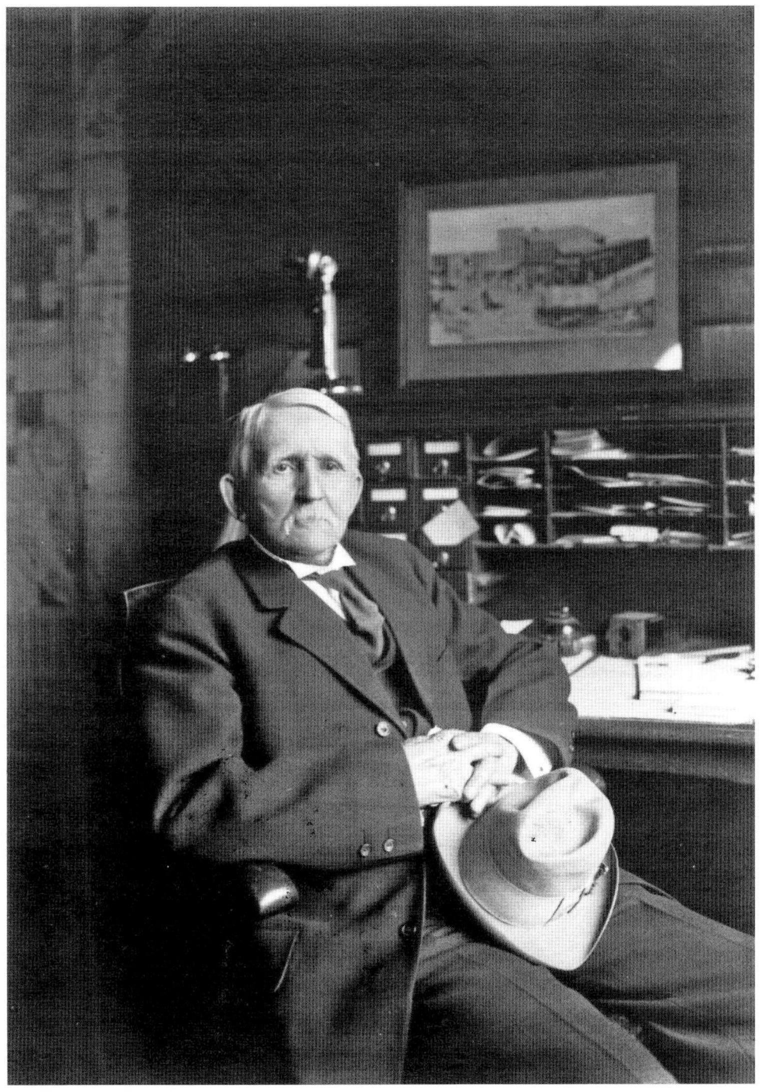

J.S. Brown. *Courtesy of the Farrington family.*

meeting that day, realizing how ill his daughter had become. The newspaper account of her death stated that although it was a heavy blow to the family, it might have been a relief to her long suffering, as she had been ill for the better part of a year.

J. Sydney remarried two years later, and his second wife, Adele, had five more children. By this time, his fortunes had increased substantially, and he built a mansion on Grant Street in Denver that was referred to as Brown's Schoolhouse. His grandson, William K. Brown Jr., related years later, "Well do I remember how Buffalo Bill Cody sat on that front porch with four or five of us grandchildren on his lap as he spun tales of his experiences."

ELBRIDGE SOPRIS WAS born in 1843. When his father headed west to explore the gold regions, Elbridge appeared in Denver a scant two months later, just a month shy of his sixteenth birthday. Young Elbridge rode horseback to the flourishing mining camps of Idaho Springs, Georgetown, Russell's Gulch and Central City to deliver news to the miners eager for contact with the rest of the world. For a time, he worked for William Byers as a printer for the newspaper.

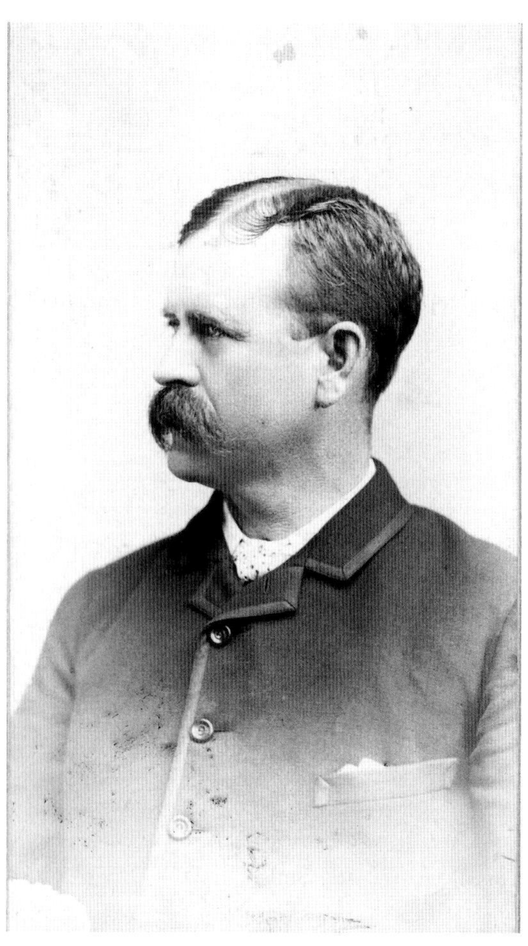

Eldridge B. Sopris. *Courtesy of the Farrington family.*

When Captain Sopris organized Company C for the Colorado Volunteers, his young son enlisted and was assigned to Company A. Elbridge—or E.B., as he was known—became Colonel Slough's orderly during the Glorieta Pass campaign. He wrote to his brother shortly after the battle and remarked, "Nary Texan was to be seen,—the pills from our guns were pretty hard to take."

After the skirmish at Glorieta Pass, most of the troops either opted to go back home and resume their lives or went to fight with other Union forces in the east. Back in Colorado, the Indians alternated between trying to subsist on their substantially reduced lands and trying to take them back from the white intruders. Governor Evans and newspaperman William Byers actively used the news media to alarm the people about the Indian "threat." The governor was authorized to form a Colorado Cavalry, whose existence was to be limited to a hundred days in duration, in order to combat the danger that they believed the Indians posed. Colonel Chivington was placed in charge of the Third Colorado.

In 1864, Elbridge Sopris reenlisted as a second lieutenant in the Third Colorado Regiment. He was promoted to first lieutenant of Company A and went with Chivington's troops as they headed toward the encampment of Indians located at Sand Creek, about forty miles north of Fort Lyon. On November 24, 1864, Chivington's men attacked the Indians at Sand Creek. All were massacred—braves, women, children. Even those who thought they had agreed to a truce and held up flags of surrender.

Their victory was short lived. When the Third Colorado returned to Denver, the actual story began to emerge. Both the governor and Colonel Chivington were soundly condemned for their cruel acts against innocents, even if they were Indians.

Many years later, having eventually earned the rank of general, Elbridge was asked about his participation in the Sand Creek affair. He still maintained that "the right was on the side of the whites." He was an active member in the original Grand Army of the Republic, an organization established in 1883 and dedicated to the service of veterans and their families.

The general settled in the town of Trinidad after his military duty ended. He became a surveyor and real estate developer in that area. Also attuned to local politics, E.B. served as representative from Las Animas County in the Colorado legislature from 1885 to 1887.

In his capacity as surveyor, E.B. prepared the first plat of Trinidad and its immediate surroundings. He held royalty deeds to some of the coal land in the area that were sold to the Colorado Coal and Iron Company. The town of Sopris was established in 1886 and named in his honor. It was first called the Sopris Coal Camp, and coal mining operations began there in 1887.

In 1889, Elbridge married a widow, Mary Louise St. Vrain Skelley, and adopted two of her children. At his request, the children changed their name from Skelley to Sopris.

Mary Louise St. Vrain was the daughter of Marcellin St. Vrain and "Red," a sister of the Sioux Chief Red Cloud. Marcellin's brother was Ceran St. Vrain, one of the partners who had established Bent's Fort.

William R. Sopris, Elbridge's stepson, wrote about his grandmother, Red, with whom he had spent time during the years of his youth. He recalled many of her philosophies, among them relationships between the Indians and white settlers. While she wept over her kinsmen's defeats, she "realized and saw the hopelessness of the struggle against the whites."

William went to law school at Columbia College in New York City and returned to Denver to begin his legal career. He moved back to Trinidad in 1893. Like his adopted father, William became involved in politics and served a term in the Colorado legislature representing Las Animas County.

Mary Louise passed away in 1916. Elbridge stayed in close contact with his family in Denver. He was involved in a Memorial Day Parade there in 1929 and was asked if he wanted to ride through the parade. His answer was: "Never rode in a parade yet—never will; when I can't march, I'll stay home." He was then eighty-six years old.

On his ninetieth birthday, E.B. talked to a news reporter of the changes that had come through modern invention. "Improvements?" he asked. "We have the telephone, the automobile, the airplane, but where is our leisure, where the repose, where the privacy which made life so rich?"

General Sopris died in 1936 at the age of ninety-two, having outlived the rest of the eight brothers and sisters.

SIMPSON SOPRIS WAS born in 1845 and was but fourteen years old when his family first arrived in Denver. He went to work in 1860 for the *Rocky Mountain News*, starting as a "devil"—an apprentice in the printing office. He worked his way up through various positions until he was in charge of the business department of the office. He was thinking of a career in journalism but instead joined his brother-in-law J. Sydney Brown at the J.S. Brown Brothers Mercantile.

Sim, as he was known, donated a gateway arch that was erected in 1912 at the 17th Avenue entrance to City Park. The Richard E. Sopris Gateway, at a pedestrian and trolley entrance, highlighted the many accomplishments of Sim's father.

Then in 1925, he donated another memorial, this time to his mother, Elizabeth Sopris. The statue of a small boy with a bronze sundial at his feet is located just west of the park's pavilion.

In February 1928, Sim wrote an article, published in *Colorado Magazine*, entitled "Santa Fe Drive, Denver." Sopris describes how a street formerly known as Jason Street was renamed Santa Fe Drive. He goes on to tell how his family's home was then on Ferry Street and that "a path led from the front gate of our place directly down to the traveled part of Ferry Street."

A footnote to the article explained that "he has written for the State Historical Society a number of historical sketches which are original source material."

In August of the same year, Simpson Sopris passed away after a month's illness.

HENRY SOPRIS WAS born in 1847 and was about thirteen years old on his arrival in Denver. Sadly, the newspaper reported his death in December of 1870, when he was only twenty-three years old. "The death of their son Henry is not unexpected, but not the less trying" for the family of Captain Richard Sopris.

LEVI SOPRIS WAS born in 1850 and had reached the age of ten years when the family came west. He attended school in Denver as he grew up.

Known as Lee, he went to work as a guard at the county jail when his father was the jailor there. There were two major jailbreak incidents during the early 1870s, the second of which Lee barely survived.

There is record of his having married Victoria Mayberry in October 1887 in Garland, Arkansas.

In 1893, when his father passed away, Levi was recorded as "having lived in Hot Springs, Arkansas, for the past five years."

Back in Denver, he was on record in 1901 as having been selected as a juror for a court case. When questioned by the attorneys, he stated that he "never reads the newspapers" and had no knowledge of the case being tried. He listed his occupation as formerly a farmer but now doing nothing.

The next record available of Levi was a short notice in the *Rocky Mountain News* in June 1913 of his death in Paris, Texas.

THE YOUNGEST OF the Sopris children was George, who had been born in 1853, thus had attained the age of seven years when his family arrived in Denver.

In 1863, after his father had returned from military service and the family was living on their farm near Clear Creek, George was the victim of a gunshot accident. He had been playing at the house of a neighbor when a loaded shotgun went off, shattering George's right hand and wrist and doing damage to his nose, cheek, lip and eye. The *Rocky Mountain News* reported that Dr. Clark administered chloroform and amputated George's arm midway between his elbow and wrist.

The diary of his sister Indiana, however, refuted the report. Apparently Dr. Clark had been replaced by Dr. Hamilton, who decided that George's arm could be saved without amputation. A few months later, Indiana wrote in her diary, "Brother George came to stay with us and go to school. We ought to be more resigned than we are but I feel terribly when thinking of his future. I am afraid he will lose his cheerfulness when he goes among the boys and sees how little he can do."

Contrary to his sister's fears, George's injury seemed not to affect his ambitions. He went from Denver schools to study law in the offices of Belden & Powers and was admitted to the bar in 1875. He held a number of offices during his lifetime: justice of the peace, county commissioner, superintendent of the census, police magistrate and public trustee.

He lived to the ripe age of seventy-five before his death in 1929. He never married and was still living at the family home at 1337 Stout Street. He had outlived all of his brothers and sisters except one—E.B.

14
Sopris the Town

The town of Sopris was a coal town. Before coal began to be a commodity, there was a Spanish settlement there, known as Carpiosas, located about four miles southwest of Trinidad on the south river bank of the Purgatoire River. Elbridge B. Sopris had come from Indiana, fought with the Colorado Volunteers at Glorieta Pass and settled in the Trinidad area. He was an early surveyor of Trinidad and the area near it. The town was named in his honor.

Originally established in 1886 by the Denver Fuel Company, Sopris officially became a coal town when its first coal mine was opened in 1887. The town was platted in 1888. The owner of the fuel company reorganized all of his coal company holdings into the Colorado Fuel Company (CFC). By the end of the decade, the Sopris Mine had become the state's largest coal producer.

The CFC and another coal-producing company, the Colorado Coal and Iron Company, had been in cutthroat competition with each other. In 1892, they decided to merge and gained stockholder approval for the merger. Thus the Colorado Fuel and Iron Company (CF&I) was created.

There are three major grades of coal. Anthracite is the most dense, and although it is difficult to ignite, it burns the most cleanly. Lignite is a softer grade of coal, containing much organic matter, therefore easier to ignite. It was used for domestic fuel. The middle grade is bituminous, which was the type found in Sopris and other Colorado coal communities. Bituminous coal was often purified into coke, which involves baking the coal slowly without igniting it to remove organic impurities.

Railroads were big users of the bituminous coal produced. The Denver & Rio Grande Railroad, looking for ways to operate more efficiently, thought that producing the steel for the rails locally would save it money. The Colorado Coal and Iron Company had been formed for this purpose. A steel mill was built in Pueblo in 1879 and became the other big user of the bituminous coal produced locally.

The company town was developed to attract workers whose lives and those of their families then became part of their jobs. No other transportation was required, as the miners would easily walk to work. And no other transportation was required for the wives and children, as their shopping and schools were also within walking distance. The communities became close-knit as the families supported one another. And when they weren't working (which wasn't often), they developed recreational activities among the families.

But the company town concept is a double-edged sword. The company had complete control of their lives. And if the workers or their families protested, the company had the option of simply cutting them off from major services. The lyrics of a country song, "I owe my soul to the company store," told that story very plainly and made Tennessee Ernie Ford quite popular as he sang and recorded "Sixteen Tons."

But life wasn't all bad in the company town. While ethnic cultures tended to settle in America close to those from their own origins, in a coal town, you had to live intimately with those of all cultures. The town of Sopris was populated mostly by those of Mexican and Italian descent. Most of them were Roman Catholics, so their religious beliefs provided a common denominator. But they all worked and played together.

The community seemed to have been planned at the outset rather than cobbled together, as in other towns. The town had neat rows of two-story duplexes and a number of single-family dwellings. The streets were lined with same size trees equally spaced on both sides. Although the streets were not paved, they were adequate for the horse and wagon transportation that was prevalent, and most of the residents walked wherever they needed to go. Eventually, a trolley system was established to carry residents to Trinidad and back.

Favorite pastimes included picnicking, baseball games and families spending time together for meals. And of course there were the requisite number of saloons. During prohibition years, when the saloons couldn't legally sell liquor, people brought out their recipes for homemade hooch of one kind or another. Company officials wisely tried to contain rather than prohibit the consumption of alcohol. The miner's lunch bucket was packed in the morning with fresh water and food for the day. After the end of his shift, the miner would often stop at a saloon and fill his bucket with beer, which cost the grand sum of ten cents.

Those who lived in Sopris in 1915 were recovering from the memory of the devastating coal strikes in 1913 and 1914 in neighboring Ludlow. John D. Rockefeller, whose family owned 40 percent of the stock of CF&I and had been considered one of the enemies of the miners, visited Sopris that year. Rockefeller made it a point to live, eat and sleep with the miners during his trip there. He was remembered by many of the youngsters for his habit of giving away dimes to them. In spite of their poverty, a number of them kept the dimes as a memento from the only multimillionaire they would probably ever meet.

The Rockefellers were known for their establishment of YMCA quarters, and in Sopris they built a permanent band shell along with a YMCA for use by the local people. The YMCA became a center of activity in Sopris. Eventually, it was donated by CF&I to the high school, where it served as a gymnasium, affectionately dubbed the "crackerbox." It was not only a place for sports activities but was the building that was used for a movie theater, a dance hall, a wedding reception and any other event that required seating for a large number of people.

The demand for coal began to wane after World War I as petroleum gradually became the fuel most widely used. During that period, Sopris had a population of nearly 2,000, and about 650 men were employed at the mine.

In 1928, after having produced over nine million tons of coal, the Sopris Mine was abandoned by CF&I. Limited mining operations continued until 1940, when it was found that the coal veins were completely exhausted. After that, the town of Sopris continued to exist as a small retirement community.

Citizens of the town of Trinidad, meanwhile, had become tired of the springtime rampages of the Purgatoire River and approved a project through the 1958 Flood Control Act to create Trinidad Lake. The U.S. Army Corps of Engineers planned and built the dam that would provide flood control, irrigation and recreation for the public.

By the time the Army Corps of Engineers had finished building the dam in 1970, there were only three hundred residents left in the town of Sopris. It became obvious that they had to move as the waters began to fill the reservoir. Since the town had never been officially incorporated, the government was not obligated to find them new homes. They were simply paid a bit of money and told to move, and then their homes were bulldozed into piles of rubble.

And so Sopris, one of the oldest and most productive coal towns in Las Animas County, now sits at the bottom of Trinidad Lake.

15
State Historical Society

Not long after his election as mayor of the city of Denver, Richard Sopris was again involved in establishing an organization that was to have lasting impressions in the city, as well as in the state of Colorado. In January of 1879, a bill was introduced in the Colorado House of Representatives: "an act to encourage the formation and establishment of a State historical and natural history society."

> *Whereas, the history of Colorado, being as yet unwritten, and existing now only in tradition or fragmentary manuscripts of private individuals and of the public press; and*
> *Whereas, the natural history of Colorado, as represented by published essays of scientists and by preserved specimens, is set forth only by organizations and museums without the state, in this country and in Europe; and*
> *Whereas, the opportunity, now so evident, for making a permanent record of these essential elements of our prosperity, is fast passing away, so that a few years hence, both the men who have been the actors, and the material for collections, will be quite beyond our reach; and*
> *Whereas, it is believed that many valuable historical papers, and specimens of our natural history, would be contributed to a properly organized society; therefore, in order to encourage and promote the advancement of these material interests, and to establish a state museum—*

The act went on to establish initial rules and provisions for the organization. It was approved on February 13, 1879.

William D. Todd, a member of the House of Representatives, was credited with taking initiative on the bill. Todd became the treasurer of the society, a position that he filled for twenty-six years. A committee was appointed to draft articles of incorporation for a permanent organization. One member of the committee was Richard Sopris.

The constitution and bylaws of the organization provided for officers: a president, four vice-presidents, a corresponding secretary, a recording secretary, a treasurer and a board of curators. Richard Sopris was elected as one of the first two vice-presidents.

The first bimonthly meeting of the Colorado State Historical and Natural History Society was held in the Supreme Court Room on September 15, 1879, and the address of the evening was to be given by Mayor Sopris. The Mayor had been called elsewhere for the evening, but his address was read by Todd. A portion of it was printed in the *Rocky Mountain News*:

> *Denver's rise and progress are a marvel of modern civilization. Situated on a great desert, beyond the frontier, six hundred miles from civilization, during the dawn of a fierce rebellion, and in the heart of an empire of Indians, who were hostile on every side, Denver has a right to be proud of its present glorious progress. Here, where eighteen years ago there were scarcely thirty white men, we to-day can boast of a magnificent metropolis, with a population of thirty thousand. The early "pioneers of bravery" sought the junction of Cherry creek with the South Platte, as a "promised land" of gold. Previously this section of country was known in geography as the "Great American Desert," and in civil government as Arapahoe county, territory of Kansas. Indeed, it was known as the "Great Unknown" by the national conventions of that day. Closely following the panic of '57 the reports of gold in the Rocky mountains spread like wild fire in the west and south, causing a general rush to this territory as early as the summer and fall of 1858.*
>
> *IN CONCLUSION*
> *The history of the town was traced from that old territorial time down to the time when the present metropolis of the mountains had been recognized as a place of some considerable pretensions. From that season to the present, our young and beautiful queen of the plains progressed from year to year with improvement and enterprise upon enterprise, schools, churches, business*

> *marts, private palaces, city water works, city gas works, city street cars, a gallant fire department, and last but not least, statehood, until now she is empress of all the surveyings from the father of water to the Golden Gate of the Pacific.*

At the next meeting in November, a paper was presented by Professor Gove on the Schools of Denver, which incidentally included mention of Denver's first woman teacher, Indiana Sopris.

The society began to publicize its need for specimens suitable for the museum. Members appealed through the press to miners, mine owners and prospectors to contribute to the cause. By 1881, the society had listed donations of minerals, rodents, birds, newspapers and books, as well as presentations from local personages about Colorado history. A few years later, the list had grown to include mounted and preserved specimens of fauna and flora, minerals, coins, Indian relics, fossils and skeletons, as well as historical papers and books.

Will C. Ferril became the first paid official of the society in 1896, as he assumed the duties of curator. Ferril had been a teacher, a lawyer and a journalist, serving as editor of several Denver newspapers. Upon his appointment as curator, Ferril immediately began an educational program, encouraging teachers to bring their students to the museum to study its exhibits.

William N. Byers, editor of the *Rocky Mountain News* from 1859 through 1878, became president of the society upon the resignation of Dr. Bancroft in 1896. With two noted journalists at the helm, it was inevitable that a campaign began to collect copies of local newspapers and publications for use in the museum as historical source materials.

The society had created a separate Division of Natural History, which was active through 1898. Children were invited to study the bird collection with over five hundred specimens, as well as the artifacts from the Cliff Dweller Collection. Then in 1899, a group of prominent citizens created the Colorado Museum of Natural History as they negotiated the purchase of the entire collection of Edwin Carter, a naturalist and taxidermist. The new museum later became the Denver Museum of Natural History, located within Denver's City Park.

The society eventually became the State Historical Society of Colorado, relinquishing the "natural history" part of its name. It is now known as History Colorado.

The historical society continued to collect books, pamphlets, diaries, maps, photographs, biographical sketches and family histories, as well as

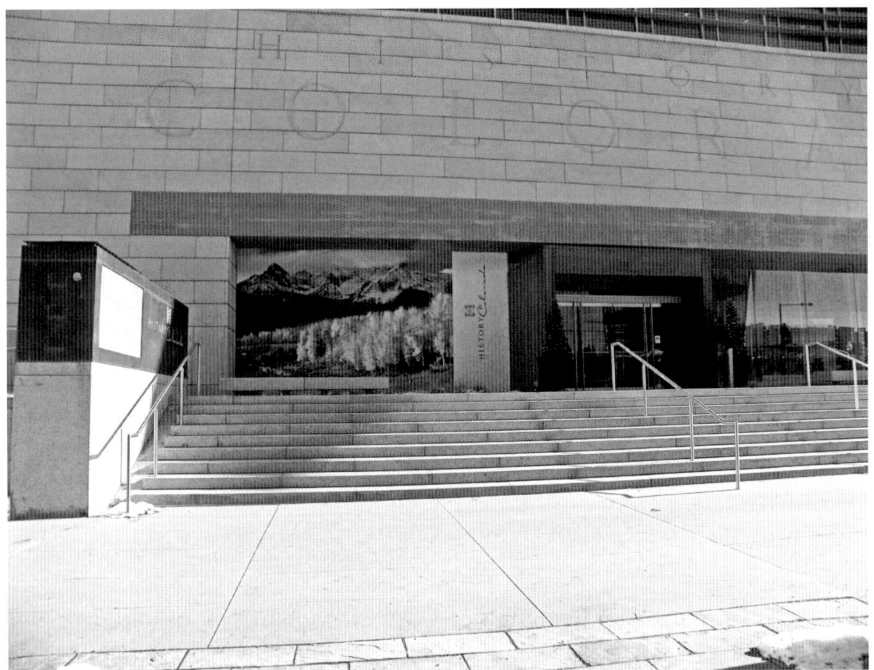

History Colorado. *Author's collection.*

any other documentation that added to the collection of Colorado history records. Materials were donated by the Sopris family: portraits of Captain Sopris and E.B. Sopris; a scrapbook of Captain and Mrs. Sopris' golden wedding anniversary records; an 1859 Denver business directory; and 1876 and 1877 maps of Colorado among other items.

Richard Sopris bore many titles during his lifetime, but the one that seemed to stick throughout was "Captain." From the time he first appeared in the fledgling town that became Denver, Captain Sopris was involved in almost every step of the progress of his adopted state, particularly the city that he labeled "Queen of the Plains."

16

And the Family Tree Grows

Irene Cushman, granddaughter of Captain Richard Sopris and daughter of Indiana Sopris Cushman and Samuel Cushman, was the firstborn of the couple, who was now living in Deadwood, South Dakota. She grew up

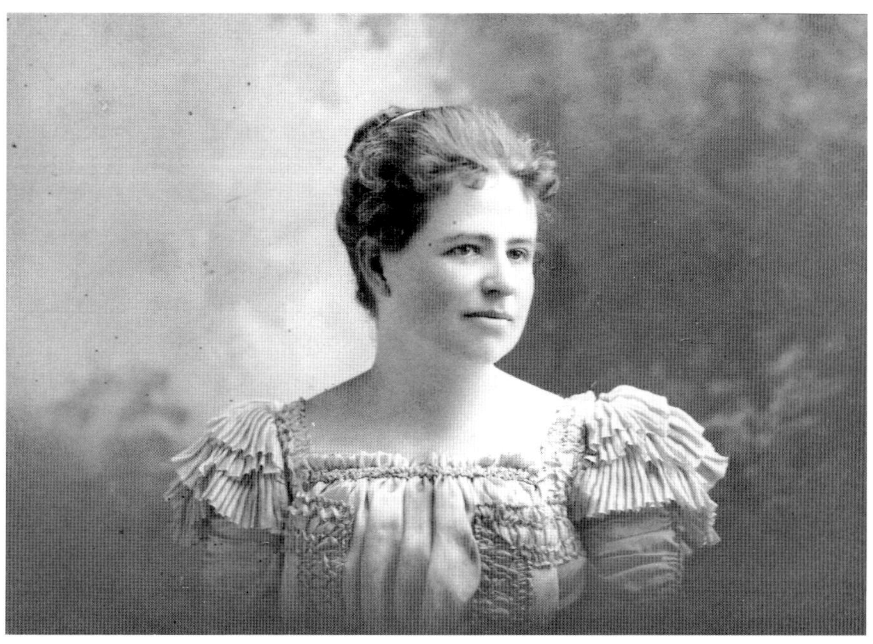

Irene Cushman. *Courtesy of the Farrington family.*

in Deadwood and was a member of the first graduating class of six in that town in 1886. She went to Massachusetts to attend the Lassell Seminary for a year.

The Territory of Dakota was organized in 1861 and consisted of the northernmost part of the land acquired in the Louisiana Purchase. Although approved early in Abraham Lincoln's presidency, the Dakota Territory had very little involvement in the Civil War. Even while battles were still being fought, expeditions were authorized into the territory and protective forts were built along the Missouri River. This was the path traveled to the Pacific Coast and the lucrative fur trade. As railroads were built, settlers moved westward and the population increased. Individual states began to split off. Montana, Wyoming, North Dakota, South Dakota and a bit of Nebraska made up the original Dakota Territory; by 1868, it was down to the two Dakotas. In 1889, the remaining Dakota Territory was divided into two states: North and South Dakota.

Irene was twenty-two years old when South Dakota emerged as a state. The next year, she began to keep a diary. She named it her "book" and confided her thoughts, feelings and aspirations to it often. During the year 1890, she wrote of her life in Deadwood, which seemed to be full of parties, dances, church activities and involvement with other young men and ladies. She referred to them as "y.m." and "y.l." Her book began to show entries involving a certain "a.d.w." This was a y.m. whose full name was Albert Daniel Wilson.

Wilson was then a superintendent of the Deadwood Central Railway, and his job took him out of town frequently. When he returned to town, he always looked forward to dancing with a certain young lady—their favorite dance was the waltz. While they were seeing each other off and on, he was referred to in her book as "Ady." They had a somewhat tumultuous relationship during that year. Irene couldn't seem to make up her mind between a.d.w. and another fellow she was keeping company with. Wilson fell head over heels in love with her and was often frustrated when he saw her in the company of his rival. When he finally got the courage to propose to her, she told him that she couldn't make up her mind between the two of them, saying that she had strong feelings for each of them. When she was with one, she liked him; and when she was with the other, he was her preference.

Wilson finally reached the end of his patience. He asked Irene for all his letters to be returned to him, as he could see no future for them. Irene pondered this for a day or two and decided that she really didn't want to return his letters. So she made her decision, and the entries in her book were now full of affection and plans for their wedding. And she began to refer to him in her book as "Allie."

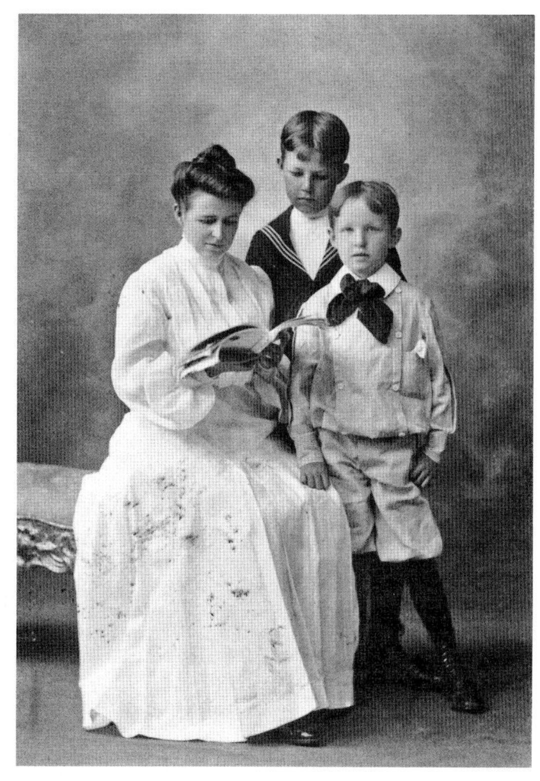

Irene Cushman Wilson and children. *Courtesy of the Farrington family.*

The wedding took place on October 8, 1891, at the home of Irene's parents in Deadwood. The maid of honor was Charlotte, Irene's sister, and the best man was George, Irene's brother. The newlyweds left for a two-week honeymoon in Chicago as they were showered with rice by enthusiastic guests. A year later, their first son, Arthur Cushman Wilson, was born. Irene stayed in Deadwood with her eight-month-old child when her mother and sister went to Denver in April 1893 to attend her grandfather's funeral. In 1896, a second son, Sidney Evert Wilson, was born.

Irene was active throughout the rest of her life. She was the organist for the Episcopal Church, a member of the Round Table Club and was in charge of selecting books for the new Deadwood Carnegie Library. Her beloved Allie became involved in a mining and milling firm after the Deadwood Central Railroad went out of business. He was often away from home on business.

Years later, Irene picked up her "book" and made a few more entries:

> *Since these ten years have passed my dearest father has died* [1899], *and brother George died* [1903]*...both are buried in Denver where mama lives with grandma. I was not with either when they died, or when they were buried. Papa dying on the train between here and Denver and mama going on and burying him there. Sharly* [sister Charlotte] *went to the funeral. I staid here to get mama's house ready to rent furnished. When George passed away after years of suffering and mama had taken him everywhere, living 8*

months in Chicago for treatment…Grandma is still well and strong at 93 years. Uncle S.T. and Geo. are her devoted slaves, and mama.

Arthur grew up and in 1917 married Vera Bentley from the neighboring town of Lead, South Dakota. Two children were born to them—Betty Evelyn in 1918 and Sidney Bentley in 1920. Arthur Wilson worked for a time as a surveyor for the South Dakota Highway Department and then served in the U.S. Army for a brief period at the end of World War I. He and his family lived at his parents' home after his mother's death in 1922.

After his wife Irene's passing, Albert went to live in Florida, where he started a fish packing business in Bonita Springs on the Gulf Coast. Arthur took his family to West Portal, now called Winter Park, in Colorado, when he found a job as warehouse foreman during the construction of the Moffat Tunnel. The Great Depression wreaked havoc for many people in those days, and the year 1928 found Arthur without a job, so he, Vera and their children joined his father in Florida. While in Florida, Arthur took a test to work for the Colorado State Highway Department. He passed the test with the highest rating on the list and was offered a job back in Colorado. The

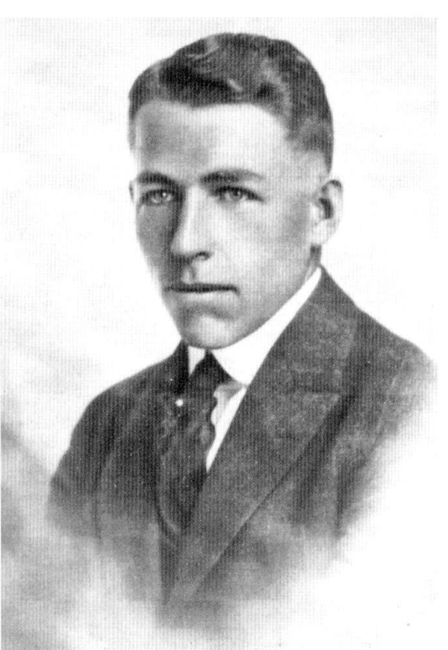

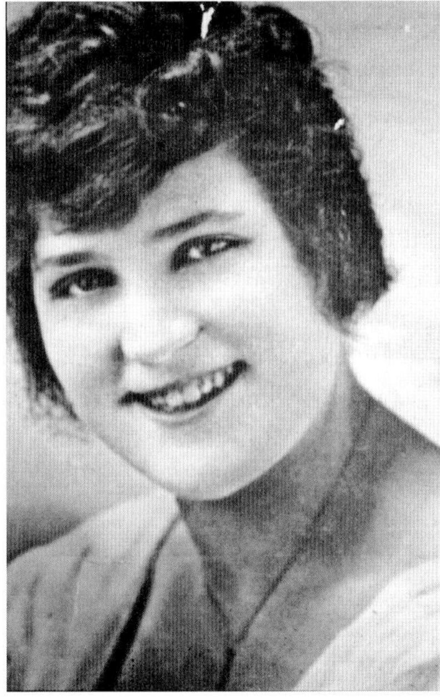

Left: Arthur Wilson. *Courtesy of the Farrington family; right*: Vera Bentley Wilson. *Courtesy of the Farrington family.*

family lived for a time in Denver, then moved to the little town of Grant. The year 1931 found the family back in Denver, and finally in 1932, they were transferred to Buena Vista.

Betty Evelyn Wilson recalls some of her earliest memories. She remembers hiking with her grandfather in the hills of South Dakota. She recalls living in West Portal and having to make a path in the snow to get to school or a store. She hated the long underwear that always had to be worn underneath long black stockings. She fondly remembers their Old English Sheepdog named Wuzzy. When the family went to live in Florida, Wuzzy went, too. As they went to the beach to swim one day, they forgot Wuzzy. When they went back to find him, he was desperately running after them along the beach with ocean waves in the background. After a number of moves, the family was finally able to settle in the town of Buena Vista.

Betty attended Buena Vista High School until her graduation in 1936. A fellow named John Farrington, nicknamed "Bus," was in the same graduating class. The two were high school sweethearts. There were actually three Farrington brothers—John, William and Bruce.

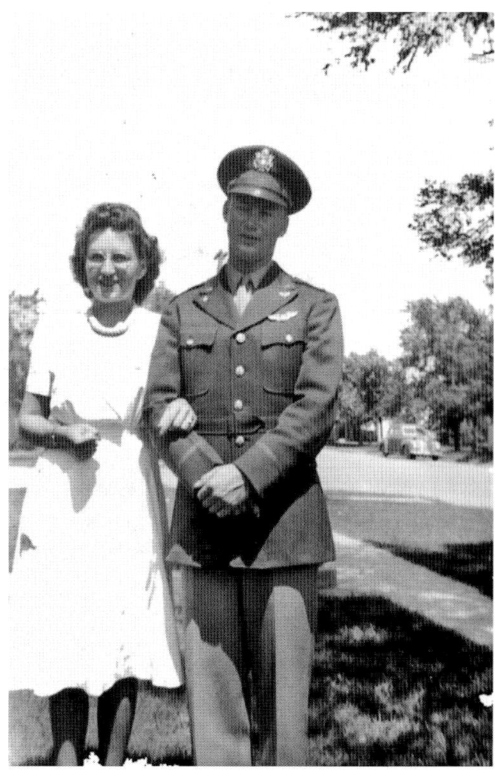

Betty and Bus Farrington on their wedding day. *Courtesy of the Farrington family.*

Betty had earned a scholarship to attend Colorado University in Boulder and studied there for a year. She taught the first through eighth grade kids at the Gas Creek School located between Buena Vista and Salida, then returned to college to finish her degree. Bus also attended college at Boulder, but his dream was to be a pilot. He was working at the Gates Rubber Company in Denver when he enlisted in a pilot training program lasting thirty weeks and graduated from the Gulf Coast Army Air

Forces Training Center. The high school sweethearts married in August of 1942, shortly before Bus' graduation as a pilot.

In October of 1943, Captain Farrington was assigned to a heavy bombardment unit as the operations officer. The unit was sent to a small base in northern Australia, next to a "kangaroo waterhole." The squadron was made up of flight crews waiting for missions to fly. October in Australia is a hot time of the year, and several of the young fellows were reminiscing about home and wishing for a cold beer.

Bus and his partner, Captain Hadley, took matters into their own hands and went foraging. They soon encountered a rancher who had run out of smokes and was willing to make a trade. For four packs of cigarettes, they brought back ten sirloin steaks and two cakes of ice from the rancher's meat cooler. As they returned to camp, they discovered that other improvising fellows had obtained the beer. So the beer was put on ice and a fire started. The feast was supplemented with potatoes and bread.

Not long after the memorable picnic, they got orders for a mission. The target was Pomalaa, a nickel-producing town in the Celebes Islands, a 2,100-mile flight. A number of bomber planes took off from their base in Australia, but due to mechanical problems, their number was reduced to four.

In the tradition of military pilots, their planes were given affectionate names. The B-24 bomber piloted by Captain Farrington had been dubbed "Fyrtle Myrtle" because not only had the captain just learned that he was to become a father but his navigator had just welcomed a new baby into his family. According to other pilots, Bus was well liked, as was his navigator, whose nickname was "Porky" because he was short and fat but good humored. Bus was nicknamed "Mother" because of the way he took care of his crew.

Another of the four planes was named the "Golden Gator," after the U.S. port that they had left. One of the few survivors from the Golden Gator later told the story of what happened to the planes on that fateful mission. The four planes had reached their target at Pomalaa and successfully scored hits on a four-thousand-ton ship in the harbor, as well as nearby mine equipment and docks. They had gone into a tight diamond formation and were headed back to Australia.

Then they encountered about fourteen Japanese fighter planes. The Fyrtle Myrtle was in the left wing position and was the first hit. One of the motors caught fire, and the plane went into a steep dive. The Golden Gator followed it down, hoping the pilot of the Myrtle could pull the plane out of its dive.

The crew of the Golden Gator heard Captain Farrington radio, "Go ahead home; you can't do us any good." Then they watched as seven men crawled out of hatches and parachuted into the sea. Seconds later the plane exploded. The Golden Gator had become separated from the other two bombers and tried to escape the Japanese by flying into the clouds. Unfortunately, the Japanese planes found the Gator and a battle ensued. The Golden Gator emptied all of its remaining munitions onto the enemy fighters, but it was outnumbered. The pilot, by then mortally wounded, told the crew he was going to land the plane on the water and they should put on their lifejackets, find the life rafts on board and get through the escape hatches.

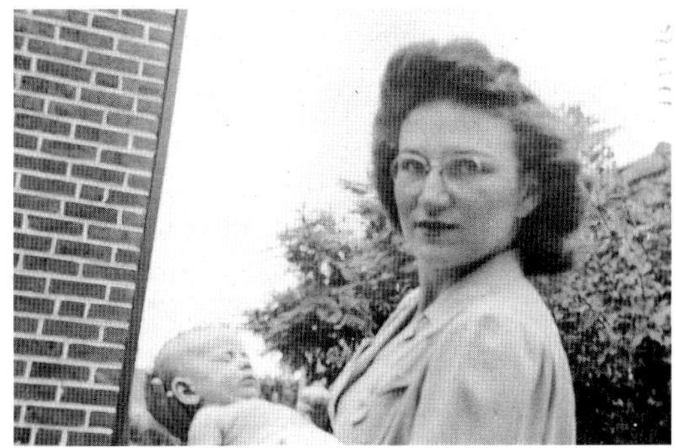

Betty Farrington and baby John. *Courtesy of the Farrington family.*

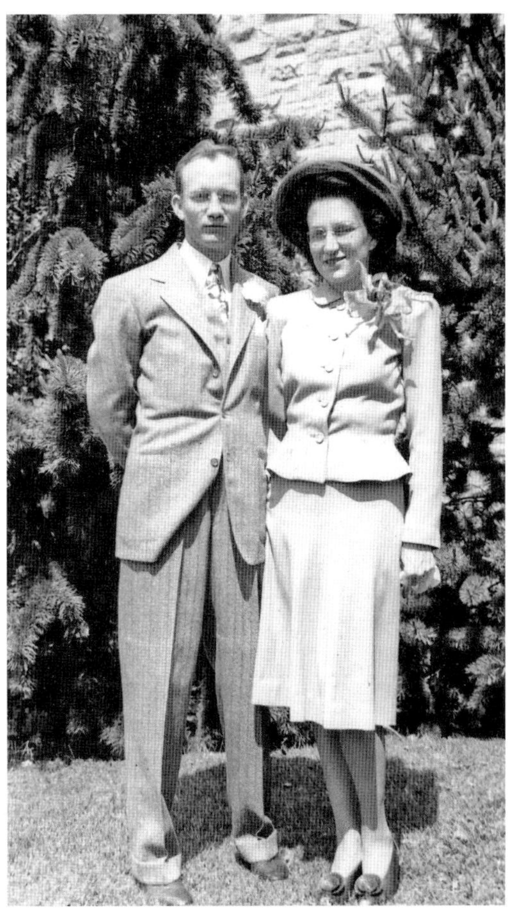

Betty and Bill Farrington on their wedding day. *Courtesy of the Farrington family.*

The Japanese fighter planes took another pass, strafing as they went. Now the survivors were adrift at sea. Out of the eleven original crew members of the Golden Gator, only four were left. All four of the men were injured, unable to help one another. On the second morning at sea, an Australian Liberator plane flew by, spotted the men in the rafts and dropped them water. The Australians then sent out a Catalina flying boat to rescue the wounded survivors. They were pulled aboard the boat and given tea, and their injuries were treated.

Of the crew of the Fyrtle Myrtle, four were rescued by Japanese fishermen. They spent the duration of the war as Japanese prisoners of war.

Notice was sent to the families of those known to be lost. Betty Farrington got a telegram where she was living in Denver that Captain Farrington had been lost at sea. Two months later, their son was born. He was named John, after his father. Betty lived with her mother in Denver for a while, then went to Colorado Springs to live with her mother-in-law. She worked at Camp Carson (now Fort Carson) in the office of the Clothing and Equipment Repairs shop. German prisoners of war worked there, too, and often showed their affection for the toddler whose daddy had been lost at sea.

Bus' brother Bill had also enlisted in the war and served in the European theater. When Bill was discharged from the service, he came to visit his family. He and Betty became close and, after a while, married. They had a daughter, Margaret. Eventually, they moved back to Buena Vista, where the Farrington brothers and Betty had gone to high school.

Betty had been a schoolteacher, and her daughter Margaret (Peg) had become a schoolteacher. As they researched their family history, they discovered the stories of Richard Sopris, who had been the mayor of Denver, and Indiana Sopris, who had been recognized as the first woman schoolteacher in Denver.

They both still live in Buena Vista, where Betty is active in the Republican Women organization, a retired teacher's society and her sorority, Delta Kappa Gamma. But one of her favorite pastimes is to play Friday night bingo at the local American Legion Hall. Recently, the patrons at bingo joined together to sing "Happy Birthday" to Betty to celebrate her ninety-seventh birthday.

Bibliography

Chapter 1

"Bucks County, Pennsylvania, Historic Fun." www.visitbuckscounty.com.

"Capt. Richard Sopris." www.findagrave.com.

Hall, Frank. *History of the State of Colorado*. Vol. 4. Chicago: Blakely Printing Company, 1895.

"A History of Steamboats." www.samusace.army.mil/Portals.

Portrait and Biographical Record of the State of Colorado. Chicago: Chapman Publishing, 1899.

"Richard Sopris." www.myheritage.com.

Rietsch, Pam, Ted Miller and Carole Miller. "Portrait & Biographical Record—Denver & Vicinity." www.memoriallibrary.com/CO/1898DenverPB.

Spangenburg, Ray, and Diane K. Moser. *The Story of America's Canals*. New York: Facts on File, Inc., 1992.

The Story of America. Pleasantville, NY: Reader's Digest Association, Inc., 1975.

Ward, Josiah M. "Why Mt. Sopris and Sopris National Forest." *Denver Post*, March 6, 1921.

Wikipedia. "Riverboat." http://en.wikipedia.org/wiki/Riverboat.

———. "Whitewater Canal." http://en.wikipedia.org/wiki/Whitewater Canal.

CHAPTER 2

Baldwin, Mark. "Mountain City." http://www.gilpintram.com/mountain_city.

Brown, Robert L. *Central City and Gilpin County: Then and Now*. Caldwell, ID: Caxton Printers, Ltd., 1994.

———. *Ghost Towns of the Colorado Rockies*. Caldwell, ID: Caxton Printers, Ltd., 1971.

Eberhart, Perry. *Guide to the Colorado Ghost Towns and Mining Camps*. Denver, CO: Sage Books, 1959.

Gallagher, Jolie Anderson. "Notorious Mountain Charley." https://joliegallagher.wordpress.com/2011/11/26.

"Gregory Diggings—Black Hawk, CO." http://www.waymarking.com/waymarks/WM9DBW.

"Gregory's Diggings: The Richest Square Mile on Earth." http://seethesouthwest.com.Lavender, David. *The Rockies*. Lincoln: University of Nebraska Press, 1968.

Smiley, Jerome C. *History of Denver*. Denver, CO: Times-Sun Publishing Company, 1901.

Sopris, Richard. "Sopris: Settlement of Denver." Bancroft Library, 1884.

Stone, Wilbur Fisk. *History of Colorado*. Vol. 1. Chicago, IL: S.J. Clarke Publishing Company, 1918.

Wikipedia. "William Greeneberry Russell." http://en.wikipedia.org/wiki/William_Greeneberry_Russell.

CHAPTER 3

Hall, Frank. *History of the State of Colorado*. Vol. 4. Chicago: Blakely Printing Company, 1895.

Lambert, Alice. "Pioneers Recall First Fourth in City of Denver." *Denver Post*, July 4, 1910.

Lamm, Richard D. "The Fourth of July in Colorado." *Colorado Heritage* 3 (1983).

McGrath, Maria Davies. "The Real Pioneers of Colorado: John C. Moore." Denver Museum, 1934.

Rocky Mountain News. "Fire in the Mountains." June 25, 1859.

———. "Our Provisional Government." March 7, 1860.

Smiley, Jerome C. *History of Denver: With Outlines of the Earlier History of the Rocky Mountain Country, XXX*. Denver, CO: Times-Sun Publishing Company, 1901.

Sopris, Richard. "Sopris: Settlement of Denver." Bancroft Library, 1884.

Stone, Wilbur Fisk. *History of Colorado*. Vol. 1. Chicago, IL: S.J. Clarke Publishing Company, 1918.

Wikipedia. "Jefferson Territory." http://en.wikipedia.org/wiki/Jefferson_Territory.

CHAPTER 4

Ashley, Susan Riley. "Reminiscences of Colorado in the Early 'Sixties." *Colorado Magazine* 13 (May 1935): 219–30.

Collier, C.C. Recent Explorations. *Rocky Mountain News*, September 20, 22, 28 and 29; October 2, 4, 5, 11, 12 and 17, 1860.

Colohan, Earl. "Garfield County," Stephen H. Hart Library and Research Center, CWA Pioneer Interviews Collection, Richard Sopris, 1813–1893.

Kane, Willa. "Prospectors Named Sopris Peak after Leader of Expedition." *Post Independent*. http://postindependent.com.

McMechen, Edgar C. "The Model of Auraria-Denver of 1860." *Colorado Magazine* 12 (July 1935): 121–26.

Nelson, Jim. *Glenwood Springs: A Quick History*. Fort Collins, CO: FirstLight Publishing, 1998.

Noel, Thomas J., and John Fielder. *Colorado, 1870–2000 Revisited*. Englewood, CO: Westcliffe Publishers, Inc., 2001.

Rocky Mountain News. "San Juan Mines." November 1, 1860.

Sopris, Indiana. *Diary of Indiana Sopris*. March and April 1860.

Stone, Wilbur Fisk. *History of Colorado*. Vol. 1. Chicago: S.J. Clarke Publishing Company, 1918.

Ward, Josiah M. "Why Mt. Sopris and Sopris National Forest." *Denver Post*, March 6, 1921.

Wikimedia. "Green River." http://wikimedia.org.

CHAPTER 5

Smiley, Jerome C. *History of Denver*. Denver, CO: Times-Sun Publishing Company, 1901.

Sopris, Richard. "Sopris: Settlement of Denver." Bancroft Library, 1884.

Zamonsky, Stanley W., and Teddy Keller. *The '59ers: Roaring Denver in the Gold Rush Days*. Denver, CO: Stanza-Harp Publisher, 1967.

Chapter 6

"Battle of Glorieta Pass (map)." http://www.cr.nps.gov/history/online_books.

Denver Rocky Mountain News. "Resolutions of the City Council." November 9, 1860.

———. "Resolutions of the City Council." November 21, 1860.

National Park Service. "Pecos." http://www.nps.gov/peco/historyculture.

Smiley, Jerome C. *History of Denver*. Denver, CO: Times-Sun Publishing Company, 1901.

Stauffer, Dave. "Camp Weld: A Tale of Denver's Birth." https://lincolnparkhistory.wordpress.com/2014/12/09/camp-weld-a-tale-of-denvers-birth.

Stone, Wilbur Fisk. *History of Colorado*. Vol. 1. Chicago: S.J. Clarke Publishing Company, 1918.

Wikipedia. "William Gilpin (governor)." http://en.wikipedia.org/wiki/William_Gilpin_(governor).

Chapter 7

"Background on Colorado Agriculture." http://lib.colostate.edu/research.

Gease, Deryl V. "William N. Byers and the Colorado Agricultural Society." *Colorado Magazine* 43 (Winter 1966): 327–38.

Goff, Richard, and Robert H. McCaffree. *Century in the Saddle*. Denver: Colorado Cattlemen's Centennial Commission, 1967.

Lavender, David. *The Rockies*. Ch. 13. Lincoln: University of Nebraska Press, 1981.

Smiley, Jerome C. *History of Denver*. Denver, CO: Times-Sun Publishing Company, 1901.

Sopris, Richard. "From New Mexico." *Rocky Mountain News*, May 10, 1862.

———. "Sopris: Settlement of Denver." Bancroft Library, 1884.

Stauffer, Dave. "Camp Weld: A Tale of Denver's Birth." https://lincolnparkhistory.wordpress.com/2014/12/09/camp-weld-a-tale-of-denvers-birth.

Stone, Wilbur Fisk. *History of Colorado*. Vol. 1. Chicago: S.J. Clarke Publishing Company, 1918.

CHAPTER 8

Rocky Mountain News. (Cattle stealing.) June 8, 1867
———. (County roads.) August 23, 1867.
———. (Criminal docket disposed of.) May 23, 1868.
———. "District Court: January Term—Trial of Corman for the Murder of August Gallagher." January 7, 1868.
———. "District Court January Term—Trial of Corman for the Murder of August Gallagher—Second Day." January 8, 1868.
———. "Preliminary Trial of George Corman for the Murder of Cheap John." March 25, 1867.
———. "Proceedings of Arapahoe County Convention." September 6, 1865.
———. (Recaptured prisoners.) May 4, 1867.
———. (Repair county road and bridge.) August 20, 1867.
———. (Repair of Sopris Bridge.) October 7, 1867.
———. (Sopris Bridge.) October 25, 1867.
Smiley, Jerome C. *History of Denver*. Denver, CO: Times-Sun Publishing Company, 1901.

CHAPTER 9

Abbott, Carl, Stephen J. Leonard and Thomas J. Noel. *Colorado: A History of the Centennial State*. Boulder: University Press of Colorado, 2005.
City of Colorado Springs. "America the Beautiful Park." https://parks.coloradosprings.gov/explore-play/explore/parks/america-beautiful-park.
Denver Post, March 13, 1921.
Denver Rocky Mountain News, March 9, 1870; April 23, 1870.
———. "Murder of Daniel Steele at Evans." November 8, 1869.
———. "The Railway Town: Evans—Its Present and Future." November 17, 1869.
Hafen, LeRoy R. *Colorado and Its People*. New York: Lewis Historical Publishing Co., Inc., 1948.
"History of Evans, Suburb of Greeley, Colorado." http://www.greeleyhistory.org/pages/evans.html.
Smiley, Jerome C. *History of Denver*. Denver, CO: Times-Sun Publishing Company, 1901.
Stone, Wilbur Fisk. *History of Colorado*. Vol. 1. Chicago, IL: S.J. Clarke Publishing Company, 1918.

Ubbelohde, Carl, Maxine Benson and Duane A. Smith. *A Colorado History*. Boulder, CO: Pruett Publishing Company, 1982.

Vickers, William B. *History of the City of Denver, Arapahoe County, and Colorado*. Chicago: O.L. Baskin & Co., Historical Publishers, 1880.

Wikipedia. "Pacific Railroad Acts." http://en.wikipedia.org/wiki/Paific_Railroad_Acts.

CHAPTER 10

Denver Daily Times, August 6, 1874.

———. "Beer-Jerkers." April 17, 1874.

———. "Cricket" ad. January 25, 1873.

———. "District Court." November 17, 1873.

———. "Getting Their Deserts." January 18, 1873.

———. "Jail Delivery." December 8, 1873.

———. "More Chase Costs." April 14, 1875.

———. "Sentenced." December 1, 1873.

———. "Tom Mason Escapes Again." January 3, 1874.

———. "Tom Mason Re-Captured." December 20, 1873.

Hafen, LeRoy R. *Colorado and Its People*. New York: Lewis Historical Publishing Co., Inc., 1948.

Jackson Citizen. "Seven Prisoners in the Denver (Col.) Jail Overcome Their Guards." August 3, 1875.

New York Daily Graphic. "Jail-Breakers in Denver." July 28, 1875.

Ortiz, Lenny. *Denver Behind Bars*. Denver, CO: self-published, 2004.

Rocky Mountain News, December 1, 1874.

———. "The Escaped Prisoners." December 8, 1871.

———. "Escape of Four Jailbirds." December 2, 1874.

———. "Flight of the Jailbirds." July 28, 1875.

Smiley, Jerome C. *History of Denver*. Denver, CO: Times-Sun Publishing Company, 1901.

Vickers, William B. *History of the City of Denver, Arapahoe County, and Colorado*. Chicago: O.L. Baskin & Co., Historical Publishers, 1880.

CHAPTER 11

Claman, Gretchen. "A Typhoid Fever Epidemic and the Power of the Press in Denver in 1879." *Colorado Magazine* 56 (Winter/Spring 1979).

Dallas, Sandra. *Yesterday's Denver*. Miami, FL: E.A. Seemann Publishing, Inc., 1974.

Denver Daily Times. "City Election." October 2, 1878.

Denver Post. "When a Denver Mob Hung a Chinaman." June 11, 1899.

Denver Rocky Mountain News. "A Municipal Matinee." October 15, 1879.

———. "Must be a Mistake." October 8, 1879.

Hall, Frank. *History of the State of Colorado*. Vol. 3. Chicago: Blakely Printing Company, 1891.

Monnett, John H., and Michael McCarthy. *Colorado Profiles: Chin Lin Sou*. Evergreen, CO: Cordillera Press, Inc., 1987.

Ourada, Patricia K. "The Chinese in Colorado." *Colorado Magazine* 29 (January 1952).

Rockwell, Judge William. *Denver Daily Times*, October 24, 1877.

Smiley, Jerome C. *History of Denver*. Denver, CO: Times-Sun Publishing Company, 1901.

Vickers, William B. *History of the City of Denver, Arapahoe County, and Colorado*. Chicago, IL: O.L. Baskin & Co., Historical Publishers, 1880.

Waymarking.com. "Hop Alley/Chinese Riot of 1880." http://www.waymarking.com/waymarks/WM2YYY.

Wortman, Roy T. "Denver's Anti-Chinese Riot, 1880." *Colorado Magazine* 41 (Winter 1965).

CHAPTER 12

Denver Post. "Handsome New Gateway at City Park, Memorial to Pioneer." July 10, 1912.

Denver Rocky Mountain News. "Captain Sopris Dead." April 8, 1893.

———. "The Golden Wedding of Captain and Mrs. Richard Sopris." June 6, 1886.

———. "A Point on Parks." July 28, 1881.

Peters, Bette D. *Denver's City Park*. Denver: University of Colorado at Denver, 1986.

Smiley, Jerome C. *History of Denver*. Denver, CO: Times-Sun Publishing Company, 1901.

Stone, Wilbur Fisk. *History of Colorado*. Vol. 1. Chicago: S.J. Clarke Publishing Company, 1918.

CHAPTER 13

Elizabeth

Denver Post. "Mrs. E.A. Sopris is 96 Years Old." February 15, 1911.

———. "Mrs. E.L.A. Sopris, Denver's Oldest Woman, Is Dead." December 20, 1911.

———. "Mrs. E.L. Sopris, Colorado Pioneer, Dies at Age of 97." December 22, 1911.

———. "Mrs. Sopris Enjoys Her 50th Christmas Holiday in Denver." December 25, 1909.

Geni.com. "Elizabeth Sopris (Allen)." http://www.geni.com/people/Elizabeth-Sopris-Allen.

Sanford, Albert B. "Life at Camp Weld and Fort Lyon in 1861–62: An Extract from the Diary of Mrs. Byron N. Sanford." *Colorado Magazine* 7 (January 1930): 132–39.

Stauffer, Dave. "Camp Weld: A Tale of Denver's Birth." https://lincolnparkhistory.wordpress.com/2014/12/09/camp-weld-a-tale-of-denvers-birth.

Wikipedia. "Ethan Allen." https://en.wikipedia.org/wiki/Ethan_Allen.

———. "Gilbert du Motier, Marquis de Lafayette." https://en.wikipedia.org/Gilbert_du_Motier_Marquis_de_Lafayette

Allen

"Allen B. Sopris." http://www.findagrave.com.

Denver Mirror. "Clean and Fix Up." October 25, 1874.

Denver Post. "Mrs. Ellen W. Sopris, State Pioneer, Dies at Daughter's Home." April 13, 1921.

Denver Rocky Mountain News. "News from San Juan." January 17, 1861.

———. "Purchase Abbot Buggy Co." August 5, 1883.

———. "Scraps of History." November 11, 1877.

———. "Tom Tobin's Needs." March 6, 1897.

McConnell, Virginia, "Captain Baker and the San Juan Humbug," Colorado Magazine Issue XLVIII, 1971:59-75

Nossaman, Allen, "Many More Mountains," Sundance Publications, Ltd., Denver, CO, 1989:55,62-64
Rocky Mountain News. "A Store Burglarized." August 22, 1874.
———. "Death of Allen B. Sopris." May 4, 1897.
———. "From the San Juan." December 10, 1860.
———. "Funeral of A.B. Sopris." May 6, 1897.
———. "San Juan Mines." November 1, 1860.

Indiana

Aberdeen Daily News. "Pioneer Black Hills Woman Dies in Denver." September 26, 1925.
Dawson, Thomas F. "Colorado's First Woman School Teacher." *Colorado Magazine* 6 (July 1929): 126–31.
"Denver's First School Teacher Is Now Living Here with Mother." Unnamed Denver newspaper, 1899.
Flynn, A.J., and Leroy R. Hafen. "Early Education in Colorado." *Colorado Magazine* 12 (May 1935): 13–23.
"Indiana Sopris Cushman." http://findagrave.com.
Keyes, Dora Ladd. "Vignettes of Central City, Colorado." *Colorado Magazine* 30 (July 1953): 280.
McMechen, Edgar C. "The Model of Auraria-Denver of 1860." *Colorado Magazine* 12 (July 1935): 121–26.
Rocky Mountain News. "Goldrick to the Front." April 6, 1873.
"Samuel Cushman." Unnamed South Dakota newspaper, 1899.
Sopris, Indiana. *Diary of Indiana Sopris*. March and April 1860; 1863.
Wikipedia. "Caribou, Colorado." http://en.wikipedia.org/wiki/Caribiou_Colorado.

Irene

Denver Post. "Death Comes Suddenly to J.S. Brown." January 15, 1913.
Denver Rocky Mountain News, January 2 and 21, 1881.
———. "A Lamented Death." January 22, 1881.
"Irene A. Sopris Brown." http://www.findagrave.com.
"John Sidney Brown." http://www.findagrave.com.
Kohl, Edith Eudora. "Brown's Schoolhouse." *Rocky Mountain Empire Magazine* (November 7, 1948): 4

Stone, Wilbur Fisk. *History of Colorado*. Vol. 3. Chicago, IL: S.J. Clarke Publishing Company, 1918.

Elbridge

DeBusk, Samuel W. "Early Days of Trinidad." Edited by Morris F. Taylor. *Colorado Magazine* 40 (January 1963): 285.

Denver Rocky Mountain News. "General Sopris, Pioneer of '59, Dies in Denver." January 30, 1936.

Donachy, Patrick B. *Echoes of Yesteryear: Las Animas County*. Trinidad, CO: The Inkwell, 1983.

"Gen Elbridge B. Sopris." http://www.findagrave.com.

Hall, Frank. *History of the State of Colorado*. Vol. 4. Chicago: Blakely Printing Company, 1895.

Rocky Mountain News, (letter from E.B. Sopris), 26 Apr 1862:3

Sopris, W.R. "My Grandmother, Mrs. Marcellin St. Vrain." *Colorado Magazine* 22 (January 1945): 63–68.

Stauffer, Dave. "Camp Weld: A Tale of Denver's Birth." https://lincolnparkhistory.wordpress.com/2014/12/09/camp-weld-a-tale-of-denvers-birth.

Ward, Josiah M. "Captain Richard Sopris Was a Man to Whom Others Looked for Guidance and Leadership—Foremost in Pioneer Life." *Denver Post*. March 13, 1921.

Simpson

Peters, Bette D. *Denver's City Park*. Denver: University of Colorado at Denver, 1986.

Rocky Mountain News. "Off for the East." May 28, 1871.

"Simpson T. Sopris." http://www.findagrave.com.

Sopris, Simpson T. "Santa Fe Drive, Denver," *Colorado Magazine* 5 (February 1928): 113–15.

Henry

"Henry C. Sopris." http://search.ancestry.com.

Rocky Mountain News, December 17, 1870.

Levi

Denver Post. "Died." June 9, 1913.
Denver Rocky Mountain News. "Capt. Sopris Dead." April 8, 1893.
———. "Jury Selection." May 21, 1901.
"Levi S. Sopris." http://search.ancestry.com.
Rocky Mountain News. "The Escaped Prisoners." December 8, 1871.
———. "Tom Mason Escapes Again." January 3, 1874.

George

Denver Post. "Sopris Wins Plum of Public Trustee." March 6, 1906.
"George L. Sopris." http://findagrave.com.
Rocky Mountain News. "Terrible Accident." September 10, 1863.
Sopris, Indiana. *Diary of Indiana Sopris*. 1863.
Stone, Wilbur Fisk. *History of Colorado*. "Biographical, George Lane Sopris." Denver, CO: Linderman Co., Inc., 1927.
———. *History of Colorado*. Vol. 2. Chicago, IL: S.J. Clarke Publishing Company, 1918.

CHAPTER 14

Clyne, Rick J. *Coal People*. Denver: Colorado Historical Society, 1999.
Colorado Magazine. "Place Names in Colorado." Issue 19 (January 1942): 230.
Donachy, Patrick B. *Echoes of Yesteryear: Las Animas County*. Trinidad, CO: The Inkwell, 1983.
Sneed, F. Dean. *Las Animas County Ghost Towns*. Trinidad, CO: Great Escape Publishing, 2000.
Sopriscolorado.com. "Sopris, Colorado." http://www.sopriscolorado.com.
Taylor, Morris F. "El Moro: Failure of a Company Town." *Colorado Magazine* 48 (Winter 1966): 144.
Trinidadco.com. "Info on Sopris, Colorado." http://www.trinidadco.com/forum.
U.S. Army Corps of Engineers. "Trinidad Lake." http://www.spa.usace.army.mil/Missions/CivilWorks/Recreation/TrinidadLake.

CHAPTER 15

Colorado Magazine. Editorial notes. Issue 7 (January 1930): 243–4.
———. Editorial notes. Issue 11 (May 1934): 80.
———. Editorial notes. Issue 13 (July 1936): 120.
———. Editorial notes. Issue 23 (January 1946): 190.
———. "Notes from the History Section." Issue 2 (April 1925): 83.
Denver Rocky Mountain News. "Historical Society." January 16, 1881.
———. "The Historical Society." September 16, 1879.
———. "Organizing the State Historical Society." July 12, 1879.
———. "Starting Our Schools." November 11, 1879.
———. "The State Historical Society." August 1, 1879.
Hafen, LeRoy R. "History of the State Historical Society of Colorado." *Colorado Magazine* 30 (July 1953): 161–85.
Peters, Bette D. *Denver's City Park*. Denver: University of Colorado at Denver, 1986.

CHAPTER 16

Denver Post. "Denver Flyer Lost in Heroic Air Battle." February 5, 1944.
Farrington, Betty Wilson. *Betty Evelyn Wilson: My Story*. Buena Vista, CO, 2014.
———. Interviews with author, 20131–2015.
Rocky Mountain News. "At Texas Air Schools Sunday." September 5, 1942.
———. "Denverites Provide Fixin's for Feast in Aussie Wilds." October 23, 1943.
Wikipedia. "Dakota Territory." https://en.wikipedia.org/wiki/Dakota_Territory.
Wilson, Irene Cushman. Diary. February 1890–December 1891 and April 1898.
"Wilson-Cushman." Unnamed South Dakota newspaper, October 10, 1891.

Index

A

Allen, Elizabeth 12, 15, 18, 89, 91, 92, 93, 94, 104
America the Beautiful Park 74
Arapahoe County 29, 30, 31, 48, 62, 70, 112
Arapahoe County Jail 75, 76
Arnold, Dr. 37, 95, 96
Ashley, Susan 34, 35
Auraria 17, 18, 24, 31, 32, 34, 40, 48, 98
Auraria Town Company 17

B

Baker Expedition 39, 96
Baker's Bridge 65
Bates lode 23
Bennet, H.P. 30, 79
Bentley, Vera 118
Black Hawk 22, 42, 45
board of trade 70
Brookville, Indiana 12, 13
Brown, John Sydney 100, 101, 104
Buchanan, James 48, 52
Byers, William N. 23, 24, 59, 79, 80, 81, 102, 103, 113

C

Camp Weld 50, 52, 56, 93, 94
Canby, General Edward 52, 55
Capitol Hydraulic Company 31
Carr, Joel 71
Carter, Edwin 89, 113
Centennial State 79
Central City 19, 22, 23, 99, 102
Cheap John 64, 65, 66, 67
Cherry Creek 16, 17, 18, 24, 31, 45, 50, 62, 64, 79, 81, 100, 112
Cherry Creek flood 60, 81
Chief Colorow 37
Chinese 83, 84, 85
Chivington, John 49, 53, 54, 56, 103
city ditch 88
Collier, D.C. 35, 38, 95
Colorado Agricultural and Industrial Society (Colorado Agricultural Society) 59, 60
Colorado Fuel Company (CFC) 107
Colorado Territory 48, 49, 50, 52, 56, 60, 69, 70, 78
Cook, David J. 84
Corman, George 64, 65, 66, 67
Cricket Mule Robbery 76

Cummings, Alexander 70
Cushman, Irene 115, 116, 117, 118
Cushman, Samuel 99, 100, 115

D

Dakota Territory 100, 116
Denver City Ditch 31
Denver City Town Company 18
Denver Guards 49
Denver, James W. 18
Denver Museum of Natural History 89, 113
Denver Pacific Railroad 70, 71, 72, 76
Dodd's Company 52
Doyle, J.B. 34

E

East Denver 34
Enabling Act 78
Evans, Colorado 71, 72
Evans, John 56, 69, 70, 71, 72, 102

F

Farrington, John "Bus" 119, 120, 121
Farrington, William "Bill" 119, 121
Ferril, Will C. 113
First Regiment of Colorado Volunteers 49, 55
Ford, A.C. 45, 46, 52
Ford's Company 52
Fort Craig 52
Fort Garland 38, 39, 49, 95, 96, 97
Fort Lyon 49, 93, 103
Fort Union 50, 52, 53, 55, 94
Fountain Creek 73
Freeman, Thomas 46, 47
Fremont, John Charles 48, 49
Fyrtle Myrtle 120, 121

G

Gallagher, August 64. *See* also: Cheap John
Gilpin, William 34, 39, 48, 49, 50, 52, 56, 70
Glenwood Springs 37, 95
Glorieta Pass 53, 56, 102, 107
Golden, Colorado 58, 69
Golden Gator 120
golden wedding anniversary 89, 94, 114
Goldrick, O.J. 99
Grand River 35, 36, 37, 95
grasshoppers 60, 61
Greeley, Colorado 71, 72
Greeley, Horace 23, 24, 25
Green River 36, 37
Gregory Gulch 21
Gregory, John H. 20
Gregory's Diggings 20, 21, 23, 24, 25, 27

H

Hennesey, Mike 75
Hiller, Charles 75
Holtz, Edward 77, 78
Hop Alley 83, 86
Hulsey, Margaret "Peg" Farrington 121
Hunt, Alexander Cameron 30, 58
Hunt, Ellen 58

I

Idaho Springs, Colorado 21, 102
Independence Day 29
Indiana
  river steamer 14

J

Jackson, George A. 20
Jefferson Rangers 42, 49
Jefferson Territory 30, 31, 32, 40
Jernigan, Ellen 96
Jerry 35, 36
Johnson's ranch 53, 54

K

Kansas Pacific Railroad 70, 71, 72, 73
Kansas Territory 17, 18, 29, 32, 40, 98
Kozlowski's ranch 53, 54

L

La Fayette, Marquis de 92, 93
Lake Erie 12, 13
Lincoln, Abraham 48, 68, 70, 116
Lindell Hotel 34
Little Dry Creek 16
Log Cabin, the 73

M

Marion, Charles 36, 50
Mason, Thomas 76, 77
Mayberry, Victoria 105
McMurray, Mayor Thomas 89
Meryweather, Henry 88
Michigan City, Indiana 15, 96, 98
Middaugh, William 40, 42
Milleson, Elisha 56
miners' court 29
Missouri City Ditch 27
Montana vigilantes 62, 63, 64
Monument Creek 73
Moore, John C. 32
Mountain Charley 23
Mountain City 21, 22, 23, 25, 27
Mount Sopris 37

N

Nichols, Charles 17, 18

O

Ohio River 12, 13, 14

P

Palmer, William J. 73
People's Court 42, 47
People's Government 30
Persons, Joseph, Jr. 22, 23
Pigeon's ranch 53, 54
Pollock, Thomas 99
Provisional Government of the Territory of Jefferson 30, 31, 32
Pyron, Major Charles 52, 53, 54

Q

Queen of the Plains 112, 114

R

Richard E. Sopris Gateway 89, 104
Rockefeller, John D. 109
Rockwell, Judge William 80
Rocky Mountain News 24, 29, 35, 38, 55, 60, 64, 67, 71, 87, 97, 104, 105, 112, 113
Russell, Joseph 16
Russell, Levi 16, 17
Russell's Gulch 21, 102
Russell, William Green 16, 21

S

Sand Creek Massacre 56, 103
Sanford, Mary 93, 94
San Juan Mines 39, 95, 96
Sibley, General Henry Hopkins 50, 52, 55
Skelley, Mary Louise St. Vrain 103, 104
Slough, John 49, 52, 53, 54, 55, 102
Smiley, Jerome 87
Sopris, Allen B. 15, 33, 35, 37, 39, 94, 95, 96, 97
Sopris Bridge 65
Sopris, Elbridge B. 15, 102, 103, 104, 106, 107, 114
Sopris farm 57, 58
Sopris, George L. 15, 33, 100, 105, 106, 117
Sopris, Henderson & Company 23
Sopris, Henry C. 15, 105
Sopris, Indiana 15, 33, 34, 35, 94, 97, 98, 99, 100, 105, 113, 115, 122
Sopris, Irene 15, 33, 35, 92, 94, 99, 100
Sopris, James and Mary 11
Sopris, Levi S. 15, 75, 77, 78, 105
Sopris Mine 107, 109
Sopris, Simpson T. 15, 89, 91, 104, 105
Sopris, town of 103, 107, 108, 109
Sopris, William R. 103, 104

St. Charles Town Association 17, 18
Steele, Daniel 71
Steele, R.W. 30
sundial 91, 104

T

Tappan, Samuel 49
Third Colorado Regiment 103
Todd, William D. 112
Trinidad, Colorado 103, 104, 107, 108, 109
Trinidad Lake 109, 110
Turkey War 42, 49, 58
typhoid epidemic 81

U

Union Pacific Railroad 68, 69, 70, 71

V

vigilance committee 42, 45, 46, 58, 62

W

Wall, David K. 58, 59
Washington, George 11, 12, 92
Waters, Patrick 46, 47
Weld, Lewis Ledyard 50, 56
West Denver 32, 34, 48, 98
Western Wanderer 36, 37
Whitewater Canal 12, 13, 14
Williams, Beverly D. 30
Williams, Frank 62, 63, 64
Wilson, Albert Daniel 116, 118
Wilson, Arthur Cushman 117, 118
Wilson, Betty Evelyn 118, 119, 121, 122
Wilson, Sidney Bentley 118
Wilson, Sidney Evert 117
women's suffrage 78

Y

Yardley, Pennsylvania 11
YMCA 109

About the Author

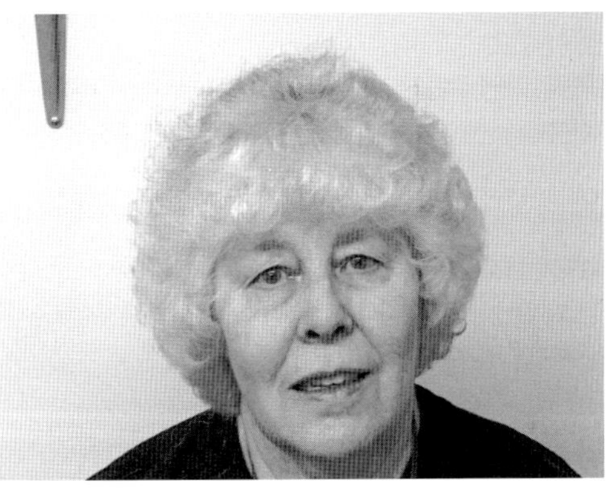

Linda Bjorklund moved with her husband to a rural mountain community in Colorado in the late 1990s to enjoy their retirement home. Although still a practicing accountant, she became interested in the history of the area and began to write about the towns and people, publishing and printing small books from her office at home. Now a widow, she continues to research local history and write. Her works include books called *Burros!* and *A Brief History of Fairplay*. She publishes a quarterly newsletter for the Park County Local History Archives and writes a monthly historical article for the *Ute Country News*.

Her interest in Richard Sopris came out of her acquaintance with one of his descendants, Betty Farrington, through the American Legion Post in Buena Vista, Colorado.

Visit us at
www.historypress.net

This title is also available as an e-book